The Saviors of God: Spiritual Exercises

by Nikos Kazantzakis

Translated, with an Introduction,

by Kimon Friar

Simon and Schuster
New York · 1960

888
K

Greetings for

Pandelis Prevelakis

from the author in Greek
and the translator in English

Contents

❂ The Saviors of God

❂ Spiritual Exercises

Introduction

The Spiritual
Exercises of
Nikos
Kazantzakis

IN VIENNA toward the end of May 1922, and in his thirty-ninth year, Nikos Kazantzakis wrote to his first wife, Galatea, in Athens, that if she were suddenly to open the door of his room, she would be filled with compassion, for she would behold him sprawled on his bed, surrounded by antiseptics, his face bound with compresses which he was forced to change every half hour. He had come down with eczema! Nevertheless, he wrote, he was reading for the first time, with patience and calm, "the wonderful theory of Freud in regard to instinct and dream." He could not eat but through a straw, he could not shave, for several weeks he had not gone out of his room except at irregular intervals when the symptoms of his malady seemed to lessen. Within a week his "eczema" had spread from his lips and chin and mounted to his eyes and forehead.

Soon all his face had puffed up until his eyes were but pinpoints in a loathsome blubber of flesh. His lower lip, swollen to many times its normal size, dripped with a peculiar kind of yellow liquid. Throughout June, July, and most of August—that is, during the remainder of his stay in Vienna—he re mained closeted in his room, because an excursion into the outer world—to a lecture, a concert, an opera—would aggravate the attack. He had no recourse but to throw himself violently into a work which had been occupying him for some time now: a verse drama about Buddha and that ascetic's renunciation of all sensory desires and temptations of the flesh. But at times despair would step through the bastions of work, and at evening, especially toward dusk, he sometimes found that he could not hold back his tears.

Neither pathologists nor dermatologists could discover the nature or cause of his disease, or help him in its cure. Yet from its inception he had met "a celebrated writer and professor of psychology at the University" who had gradually convinced him that his deformation was the result of strange psychological causes. According to this psychologist, Kazantzakis wrote his wife, his illness was the result "of a mental and spiritual disturbance which manifests itself in the body. Something like the wounds of St. Francis. He told me that I have a spiritual and mental energy beyond the normal, and that the body suffers the reaction." He complained that he had not talked to anyone for months, that he had not laughed, that he came and went—as in Buddhist narratives—alone, like a rhinoceros. "I understand those hermits now," he wrote, "who were attacked suddenly with leprosy when in their retreat they

4

reached out toward God. Skin diseases were the most usual manifestations." He had been brooding on his own ascetic inclinations, and his thoughts had become a mixture of bitterness and exaltation: "We set out from a dark point, we proceed toward another dark point—honest, clean, good—and are consoled. Because of my illness, perhaps, my soul has filled with heroic bitterness. I understand those heroes now who worked amid bodily wretchedness. To endure bitterness, yes—but at the same time, out of pride, not to enlarge your bitterness but to reach the opposite extreme—to invoke joy and health as though they were the general law. Never before have I been so prepared to perform a valiant deed as in these days when I am filled with loathing as I look on my face—bloated, wretched, with two small holes through which my glances barely pass. Dear God, if only we would not die before we have been given the opportunity to show that we are worthy of transmuting all we say into deeds!"

The psychologist had given him a book he had written in which he referred to a case exactly parallel to Kazantzakis' own. The good doctor was even planning to quote, in a future work, some remarks of his patient about *eros*, and to describe three or four of his dreams. Thus, half in bitterness and half in a form of sublimated ecstasy, he found the strength and courage to endure as long as he could work on his verse drama about Buddha, but he found it insufferable to lie in bed, changing the compresses now every few minutes, or to awaken in pain during the night. "My dear," he continued in another letter, "a mystical joy penetrates my life in this illness of mine because I am testing my endurance, because when all night long I hear the voice and laughter of men beyond my window, I do not groan, and in the early morning when the first bird quietly and timidly begins to sing within the great city, I can no longer hold back the tears of joy. It seems to me that regardless of all my harsh and evil qualities . . . something exists within me which is very kind and meek."

Suddenly, toward the end of August, he packed his bags and left for Berlin. From there, on September first, he wrote his wife: "I was made completely well, in a miraculous manner, as soon as I left Vienna." And two weeks later: "Fortunately I am still well. I hope that the Viennese psychologist was right, and that this spiritual sickness of mine passed forever as soon as I put some distance between myself and Vienna. If this is so, then it will have been a neo-ascetic case of great interest." A month and a half later he wrote that he had torn up all the three thousand verses he had written on Buddha, that he was recasting the work in a new form, into something superior, more difficult, more severe than anything he had hitherto written, into something savage and bitter. But soon after, he set aside his portrait of the Great Negator of the senses, of the "last man" of Nietzsche, and began feverishly to hack out the terms of his own salvation, his own Spiritual Exercises—to write *The Saviors of God.*[1] *

Twice, more than thirty years later, when I was collaborating with Nikos Kazantzakis on my translation of *The Odyssey: A Modern Sequel*[2]—once in Antibes in the summer of 1954, and once again in the summer of 1956 at Bohinj, near Bled, in the Yugoslavian Alps—his lower lip swelled lugubriously to great size and dripped with a yellowish fluid.

* *Notes begin on page 137.*

Pressing one soaking handkerchief after another against his lip, he tried serenely to ignore his affliction as something beneath notice, but at times his patience and his resistance would wear thin, and in one of the many moments of confidence that passed between us in work of such close and harmonious collaboration, he told me of the semantic incident which had led to his turbulence in Vienna, and which he had not revealed in his correspondence to his first wife. And he taxed me with the responsibility of making it known in time, with detachment, as "a neo-ascetic case of great interest," serene in the knowledge that, regardless of "harsh and evil" qualities in his nature, something existed within him which was very "kind and meek."

Soon after his arrival in Vienna he had gone to the theater and had found himself seated by chance beside a beautiful and charming woman. Though throughout his life Kazantzakis suffered from extreme shyness and could not even enter a restaurant without the companionable support of a friend, he found himself, somewhat miraculously, talking with his enticing neighbor. Both soon found themselves bored with the play, left together in the midst of the performance, and spent the evening walking the streets of Vienna in animated conversation. And then, to his own great surprise, Kazantzakis heard himself inviting the lady to his room; with what intention was not clear, even to himself. The lady replied that though she could not come that evening, she would be pleased to visit him on the following night. Kazantzakis went home and to bed, happy and delighted. But the next morning, when he awoke, he found his lips and chin swollen and spotted with what he first thought was eczema. He

7

sent word to the lady that he could not see her that
evening, and made an appointment for the following night; but day after day his condition worsened,
his entire face became bloated; dermatologists
could find no cause or cure for his malady, and he
continued to postpone the much-desired rendezvous. One evening, unable to bear his misery and his
imposed solitude, he attended the opera, and there
during intermission, his face almost completely
swathed in bandages, he was approached gingerly by
a stranger who inquired if he might be permitted to
ask a question. When Kazantzakis found himself
acquiescing, the stranger politely asked, "Would
you mind telling me what role eroticism plays in your
life?" Kazantzakis was taken aback and shocked,
but the stranger hastened to explain that his
question was purely clinical, that he was a professor
of psychology at the University, and that he would
look upon it as a great favor if Kazantzakis would
honor him with a visit to his office the next morning. He then apologized once more and gave his
name: Dr. Wilhelm Stekel, whose books on psycho-
pathology are known today throughout the world.

This was, of course, the anonymous professor of
psychology to whom Kazantzakis had referred in his
letters from Vienna to his wife. In the doctor's office the following morning, he found himself once
more responding easily to the doctor's frequent and
probing questions. He told Dr. Stekel that for years
he had been obsessed by the Buddhist image of life,
that now in Vienna he was struggling daily not only
to capture the essence of this vision in a verse drama
about Buddha, but that he had also resolved to live
by every Buddhist principle, to renounce the senses,
to eat sparingly, to control appetites of sight, feel-

8

ing, and sound, to abjure and to castigate the flesh. Dr. Stekel listened with amazement, and when during the course of this passionate renunciation Kazantzakis inadvertently mentioned the lady of the theater, his appointments with her and their enforced cancellations, Dr. Stekel's face glowed with unexpected understanding, and he exclaimed, "But my dear sir, this is extraordinary, extraordinary! Your malady was rather a common one in the Middle Ages, but is most rare in our own time. Indeed, I know of only one other case like it today. You have what was once called the saint's disease. During the Dark Ages many dedicated souls retreated into the sterile desert or into dark caverns, there to atone, to drain their bodies of all temptations and to castigate the flesh. Occasionally, however, when they found the temptations of flesh too much to endure, they would run howling toward town for a woman. But on the way, to their great horror, their bodies broke out in sores and boils, their faces became flushed and bloated, a yellow liquid dripped from their pores until they fell on their knees in repentance, convinced that God was punishing them for their betrayal and had stricken them with leprosy. My dear sir, you are trying to live out of your century! It is not possible to emulate the saints today! I assure you that unless you not only renounce any possible contact with your Lady of the Theater, but also leave Vienna itself, your swelling will not recede. Your body, my dear sir, is suffering from remorse of spirit." [3]

Kazantzakis listened with astonishment and disbelief, and though he continued to visit the psychologist and to read the literature he was given, he could not easily admit the psychosomatic origins of

9

his disease or that conflicts of the spirit could so deform the flesh. At the same time he continued to go stubbornly from pathologist to dermatologist, until in despair he finally packed up his bags and set out for Berlin. He told me then that to his utter astonishment, and yet with a quickening inner awakening, he felt better almost as soon as he stepped on the train, and that within an hour his swelling had receded. He professed himself baffled to understand why he suffered from similar swellings after that from time to time; yet the incident had so impressed him that he made it part of the central symbolism in many of his works, particularly in *Zorba the Greek* and *The Greek Passion*.[4] In the latter work, written in 1948, the young shepherd Manolios has been chosen to play the role of Christ in a Passion play given by his native village. But when he feels tempted to visit the widow Katerina, the village prostitute who is to play the Magdalene, his cheeks, his lips, his chin, his entire face swells up like a drum and drips with a thick and sticky liquid: "It was all bloated, his eyes were not more than two tiny beads, his nose was lost between his ballooning cheeks, his mouth was a mere hole. This was no human face, but a mask of bestial flesh, repulsive." The Pan-like, wild mountain boy Nikolio tells Manolios how his own grandfather had once tried to become a monk but had desisted because whenever he ran to the village to find a woman, he broke out in boils and leprosy, for God sent him such disease to defeat the Tempter. In *Zorba the Greek*, written in 1941–43 (but depicting autobiographically what had occurred in 1917, five years before Kazantzakis had gone to Vienna), he describes himself as a young man in his thirties filled with admiration for the uninhibited sons of the flesh, like Zorba, yet an ascetic and intellectual himself, who for years now had been writing a life of Buddha, living in a world of "compassion, renunciation, and air." He writes how the Evil One had tempted him in the shape of a woman with powerful thighs and buttocks, and how he wrote his life of Buddha in an exhausting frenzy to exorcise her image: "I wrote in what guise the Tempter had come to Buddha, how he took on the shape of a woman, how he pressed his firm breasts against the thighs of the ascetic, how Buddha saw the danger, mobilized all his powers and routed the Evil One. . . . And so I was painfully endeavoring to transform the violent desire of the flesh into Buddha." The young intellectual concludes that writing his Buddha "was no literary game but a struggle against a tremendous force of destruction lurking within me, a duel with the great NO which was consuming my heart, and on the outcome of which my life hung." [5] Kazantzakis was to take up and abandon his verse drama of Buddha from early youth till old age, and he did not publish the play in its final form until 1956.

In Berlin, during the four months between September and late December of 1922, the troubled ascetic was writing and rewriting his *Buddha*, striving by means of the purgation which poetry affords to exorcise the demon from his heart. "Buddha is the last man," he writes in *Zorba*. "That is his secret and terrible significance. Buddha is the 'pure' soul which has emptied itself; in him is the Void; he *is* the Void. 'Empty your body, empty your spirit, empty your heart,' he cries. Wherever he sets his foot, water no longer flows, no grass can grow, no child be born." And then suddenly, toward the end of December, Kazantzakis ripped away the mask of Buddha which had clung to his face so fiercely as to seep into it and deform it, and with a cry turned his real face resolutely to more naked sources, striving in an agony that characterized all his efforts to hew out, like Moses, the elemental principles of his life. In early August, from Vienna, he had written his wife: "I am in a hurry to publish whatever I have written till now that I may give myself completely to a new work, clearly my theology"; but as Mr. Pandelis Prevelakis informs us in his most penetrating and informative book *Nikos Kazantzakis and His Odyssey*, Kazantzakis had kept such a work in mind for eight or ten years previously, as evidenced by several of his posthumous notes.[6] In his still unpublished book of memoirs, *Report to El Greco*, Kazantzakis writes: "All my life I struggled to stretch my mind to the breaking point, until it began to creak, in order to create a great thought which might be able to give a new meaning to life, a new meaning to death, and to console mankind." His letters to his wife from Vienna had been filled with prophetic utterances of a slowly distilled vision, and now he was trying to capture it on paper: "I am writing *Spiritual Exercises*, a mystical book wherein I trace a method by which the spirit may rise from cycle to cycle until it reaches the supreme Contact. There are five cycles, Ego, Humanity, Earth, the Universe, God. I describe how we ascend all these steps, and when we reach the highest how we live simultaneously all the previous cycles. I am writing it deliberately without poetry, in a dry, imperative form. I tell you much about this because it is the last fruit of my search. When will the search end? Or perhaps my purpose is only the search itself; that is, the progression from point to point? Perhaps this is the very progression of God? The search itself—upward, and with coherence—perhaps this is the purpose of the Universe. Purpose and means become identified. . . . God is the supreme expression of the unwearied and struggling man. Oh undaunted, unhealable Searcher!"

Nikos Kazantzakis wrote *The Saviors of God* in Berlin between the end of December 1922 and the end of April 1923, and remained in that city or traveled throughout Germany until mid-January of 1924. During this period, when he was struggling to create a vision of life which might be "useful for the organization of those men who believe as I and who in similar ways confront their duty in regard to contemporary needs," the entire German nation was in an upheaval of what has come to be termed its "Years of Crisis"—the years from 1920 through 1923. Though Germany had been declared a democracy since the end of the First World War, her Republic was being violently challenged from both the Left and the Right. She had to meet the hostility of the Allies because of her inability to pay her war debts, and for making common cause with that other outcast, the Soviet Union, with whom she signed a treaty of friendship at Rapallo in April 1922. There had been an uprising of workers in the Ruhr, led by Communists, who later called for a general strike, though without success. A *coup d'etat* was attempted by the Right, and in Munich Hitler's National Socialists became the breeding ground of the Nazi movement with its inflamed nationalism and its anti-Semitism. A Communist-led riot in Hamburg erupted in October 1922, and Hitler's *Putsch* in Munich failed but a month later. On January 20,

1923, Kazantzakis wrote his wife that the lira had risen from 5,000 to 120,000 marks, that a book by Keyserling which he had wanted to buy had risen in cost from 3,000 to 72,000 marks in only one month. The occupation of the Ruhr by the French that same month dislocated the nation's entire economy and gave the final touch to the depreciation of the currency and to incredible inflation. On November 20, 1923, the mark was quoted at 4,200,000,000,000 to the dollar. The price of a single newspaper rose to 200,000,000,000 marks. The only valid medium of exchange was barter; the savings of a lifetime were suddenly wiped out, despair led to frequent food riots, and the incidence of political murders steadily rose. Despair and the threat of revolution, whether from the Left or the Right, inflamed the atmosphere.

Almost immediately after arriving in Berlin, Kazantzakis met an enthusiastic group of rebels, some of them active Communists, most of them in the arts, many of them Jewish, and so many of them expatriots (primarily dissatisfied Marxists from Russia) as to cause one of them to exclaim, "Berlin is a beautiful city except that it has too many . . . Germans!" Kazantzakis now tried to found a new periodical of the arts to be called *New Greece*, and he wrote enthusiastically to compatriots in Athens for their literary and financial support; but the publication was never to be launched. "Comrade" almost as often now as "Chérie" became the form of address in his letters to his wife. Buddha and Christ were being superseded by a new "religious" leader, Lenin, who had now become his prototype of the religious reformer. "Among the greatest and most bloody dramas which a man might scrutinize," he wrote his wife, "is the life of Lenin. From here I follow at close range all the spasms of his sorrows, his agonies, his unrelenting endeavors: he fights, gives way, attacks, tolerates the opposite of what he believes, watches his Idea being degraded by reality, publishes laws, acknowledges trade, property, money, private enterprise, etc., and attempts to engraft on the gigantic body of Russia as much new blood as it is susceptible of bearing. In perspective, or after a few generations, all compromises shall have been organized into a new creation; the entire work will then be revealed in toto, without details; all of Lenin's blood-drenched tragedy, which occurs daily, will have been confined to two or three episodes, because the work itself shall become the answer to all questions. The same thing has been true of Christ, of Buddha, of every reformer."

Amid the turmoil of national upheaval in Germany and the fevered intellectual activity of his particular group, Kazantzakis found himself once more tormented, as throughout all his life, by his admiration for action and contempt for his own pen-pushing; for his lack, he thought, of any restraining style; for his inability to transubstantiate his thought into deeds. "Dreadful questions of doubt and bitterness," he wrote from Russia a few years later, "tear at my heart. . . . I become lost amid rows of alphabetical letters, I give my heart paper to eat as though it were a goat! . . . I was not made to be a poet or a contemplative man; thoughts, words, beauty—all choke me. For a moment last night, after I had placed in harmony two sonorous verses, I was filled with joy. But almost at once nausea and contempt took possession, not of my mind or my soul, but of something more harsh,

15

more sinister, more disdainful which crouches within me, in my heart's core, and eats me." Yet a year later, struggling with his *Odyssey*, he was to say, "A perfect verse is the only salvation of the soul," and though Odysseus looks with contempt on the ineffectual young Pharaoh polishing and repolishing a few lines of verse, he thinks, "perhaps this breathless, fragile seed of kings was right, / perhaps upon this brainless earth, this mad goldfinch, / a song may stand more firm in time than brain or bronze." [7] Although Kazantzakis perceived clearly the inevitability of compromise, even for such a man as Lenin, and approved of it, he could never have given himself completely to such adjustment no matter how much he wanted to or tried. "If I were a politician," he concluded with saving insight, referring his wife to one of his violent thoughts on the social structure, "not only would I not have expressed this idea, but I would not even have had it." He struggled, therefore, with the only tools he had, pen and paper, striving to purify his style, dreaming of a new theology, a new religion of political action in which the dogmatic, teleological God of the Christians would be dethroned to be replaced by dedication to the theory of an evolutionary and spiritual refinement of matter. "When I die," he wrote Mr. Prevelakis from London in 1939, "some biographer will write that I was by nature an ascetic, with few desires, a man who lived at ease in poverty and renunciation. And no one will know that if I was reduced to becoming an 'ascetic,' this happened because it was not possible to live my true nature and because I preferred nakedness, once more, to cheap, degrading, middle-class livery."

Perhaps his ideal image of himself was as a Hebrew

prophet out of the Old Testament, like Isaiah or Ezekiel, who roamed the countryside from village to village, inflamed with the Word of God, and who combined thus in one entity both the poet and the doer, but who disdained to distort the inspiration of his electric vision into the betrayal of treacherous words. "No one will understand," he wrote Mr. Prevelakis, "that my *Spiritual Exercises* is meant to be neither a work of art nor a philosophy." He longed, it seems to me, to transmute his vision directly from spirit into living action without the distortion of any intervening medium. Even words, the tools of his trade, were barriers to communication, and despairing ever of refining them, he hacked them out like building blocks into crude but towering images. Like the painter who turns to collage for a more immediate replica of life, and in desperation glues or rivets on his canvas sand, iron, fur, flowers, bits of string, or fragments of newsprint proclaiming the world's catastrophes or its trivialities, Kazantzakis longed to glue on the blank pages of his despair sections from his own flesh, bits of his skin and bone, splinters from his fingernails, all ensanguined and smeared with his life's blood. Like the God who created him, he longed to transmute the Word directly into flesh, that flesh might in time be transubstantiated into something more spiritual, more refined than either words or flesh. His was the vain search and dilemma of the true mystic, and all his works must be considered to be the vain betrayers of his vision.

The winter was bitterly cold. He could find enough coal to heat his room for only two days out of the week. In his mental agony he often rose before sunrise and huddled in bed all day, laboriously tracing out his visionary dilemma with frozen and gloved hands. "I am writing the *Spiritual Exercises*," he wrote his wife in January of 1923. "I don't know whether or not you will like it. It is written with brevity, like a laborious fermentation, from cycle to cycle. I don't know—perhaps all these are the injunctions of a past age which I am carrying out at the moment when I have already progressed somewhat further. If I could only make the 'leap.' To leave behind me, on the other shore, my writings and my poetry, and to speak to men without judging, without shyness, without weighing every word! It seems to me that only then will I find the form wherein my spirit may breathe at ease. To speak to men, not to one or two, but to masses of men. To entwine my ideas with contemporary needs—economical, sociological, political. To speak and to move men concerning the present problems of their everyday lives. The Idea—abstract, fleshless, philosophical—cannot satisfy the flesh-eating spirit. . . . What you tell me is in truth my only worth—I struggle, I look forward like Odysseus, but without knowing if I shall ever anchor in Ithaca. Unless Ithaca is the voyage itself." "My soul," Kazantzakis was to make Odysseus cry out in *The Odyssey*, "your voyages have been your native land!" [8] And Mr. Prevelakis has put it precisely: "Just as the Odysseus of Homer went in search of his native land, the Odysseus of Kazantzakis went in search of God. . . . The first found his Ithaca, the second became the slayer of gods, searching for the true God."

For three months in Berlin, amid national panic, inflation, riots, political murders, utopian dreams and fevered conversations, his frozen fingers traced his dream, until at the end of April 1923 he wrote:

"My dear . . . yesterday I finished the *Spiritual Exercises*. Is it good? I don't know. I tried with simple words, as in confession, to trace the spiritual struggles of my life, from where I set out, how I passed over obstacles, how the struggle of God began, how I found the central meaning which regulates at last my thought, my speech and my actions. Ah! It is not as yet completely modulated, for a multitude of bad habits out of my past evolution obstruct me from moving in harmony with the stern, unyielding command of God. But I struggle, consciously now, to remain faithful to my life's essence. I find myself in a new borderland. The ultimate, the most holy form of theory is action. God is everywhere, in man, in politics, in daily life, and he is imperiled. He is not Almighty, that he might cross his hands and thus await his certain victory. His salvation depends upon us. And only if he is saved may we be saved. Theory has worth as preparation only; the critical struggle lies in the Act." [9]

The Saviors of God was first published in the July–August 1927 issue of the Athenian periodical *Renaissance*, and at the same time sheets from the magazine were bound for about three hundred pamphlets. After The Preparation with its three duties, after The March with its cycles of evolutionary movement from Ego to Ancestor [10] to Humanity to Earth, after The Vision itself, comes The Action, delineating the relationship between man and God, between man and man, and between man and nature. Throughout his life Kazantzakis tried, though abortively, to put his theories into practice. Twice he held short terms of public office, once in 1945 as Minister of National Education without portfolio, when he tried to unite various Socialist factions into one party; and once in 1919 when as Director General of the newly formed Ministry of Public Welfare he made his first trip to Russia, to the Ukraine, to carry out a national mission of restoring 150,000 uprooted Hellenes of the Caucasus to their native land (July–August). Now from Berlin he turned his eyes once more to Russia, where he hoped to embody his Vision in Action. He dreamed of learning some simple trade, such as that of carpentry, by which to earn his bread. "Thus," he wrote, "I shall work in Russia three hours every day and roam from village to village. There I shall test the Word I bring."

Like many men of sensitivity and compassion of that day, he thought of communism as a religion, yet a religion which was in danger of being submerged and distorted by materialistic emphasis. He rejected the materialistic bias of communism, but similarly rejected the dogmatic and anthropomorphic God of the Christians as equally materialistic. God, for Kazantzakis, was not an already predetermined goal *toward* which men proceed, but a spirituality ceaselessly and progressively created by nature as it evolves toward greater and higher refinement. It did not matter whether or not an inherent purpose was discernible in nature. "What is the purpose of this struggle?" he asks in the section entitled "The Vision." "This is what the wretched, self-seeking mind of man is always asking, forgetting that the Great Spirit does not toil within the bounds of human time, place, or casualty." [11] Indeed, it is the greatest glory of man that he can set himself his own purpose, and in this manner not only control but also direct the mysterious forces which create him and which might one day destroy him as a species. "Ah, if only one could die suddenly as he is serving a Purpose!" he wrote his wife from Berlin in November of 1922. "What Purpose? This earth, this starlight, do they have a purpose? What do we care? Don't ask, fight on! Let us set ourselves a Purpose, let us regulate our lives in harmony with the Purpose we ourselves have set. Then our actions and our words and our spiritual inclinations will take on unity, they will harmonize in agreement with this Purpose. And this harmony we must think of as a duty, that is to say, as a happiness." [12] A few days later he defined and italicized this purpose, a definition which was to become unshakably the cornerstone and key of all his work and thought; if it could be expressed in one sentence, it would be: "If we are to set a Purpose, it is this: *to transubstantiate matter and to turn it into spirit.*" [13] *The Saviors of God* is the distilled expression of this purpose, the Word which he naïvely thought would transform the materialistic basis of communism into spirituality. Kazantzakis was never an accepting or accepted Communist; most of his books were banned in Russia (in particular, those he wrote about that country), and though he supported the Loyalist cause during the Spanish Civil War, nevertheless, when as a reporter he visited the Republican sector during the fighting, he described the siege at Alcazar with profound sympathy for the courage and sacrifice of men who fight bravely, no matter how mistakenly, for a cause in which they believe. It must be remembered that the Communists with whom he consorted during Germany's Years of Crisis were themselves exiles from their homeland who were unable to accept the conflicting purposes of communism. Like all men of compassion, Kazantzakis approved of any social plan or faith which, he thought, might lead to the alleviation of man's physical sufferings, but he was even more concerned that no social plan or faith should stress materialistic well-being to the detriment of spiritual values. This is most clearly indicated by the statement which he placed before his text in the first edition of *The Saviors of God*: "*Spiritual Exercises* was written in Germany in 1923 in order to express the spiritual agony and the hopes of a communistic circle of Germans, Poles, and Russians who could not breathe easily within the narrow, backward, materialistic perception of the Communist Idea. Let *Spiritual Exercises* be thought of as the first lyrical attempt, the *first outcry* of a post-communistic CREDO."

Although Kazantzakis was to make four trips in all to Russia, to write a novel about it in French, *Toda Raba*, a two-volume account of his impressions, *What I Saw in Russia*, and a two-volume *History of Russian Literature*, and although he accepted the Peace Prize in 1956 and visited China on the invitation of its government in 1957, he never accepted the Soviet's materialistic bias but looked on the Russian experiment primarily as the violent and cyclical upheaval of matter from the fires of which the refined spirit springs: "Not that I have any new illusions about Russia, but because, on the whole, its soul is the deepest, darkest and most luminous, the most god-bearing soul of the world today." He saw in Soviet Russia those barbaric yet necessary forces which periodically disrupt the world, seemingly sudden mutations in the surge of evolutionary progress which either destroy previous softened and decadent civilizations or chal-

22

lenge them toward resurrection. Thus the Dorians descended on the Minoan and Mycenaean civilization, the Romans on the Greek, the Goths on the Roman, inundation after inundation in the cyclical, barbaric, and implacable progress of the world.

"I have not the slightest *illusion* about the present reality in Russia," he wrote his wife from Berlin in November 1922. "I know that her leaders do not have a clear idea of their mission, and here I have met the greatest of Russian philosophers, Sestov, and the writer Remizof, who left Russia because they were opposed, unable to bear the fearful details. But I also know that only in the warm brain of the ideologist is the Idea beautifully adjusted, pure, unsullied, without blood or mire—yet completely barren, sterile, superfluous. As soon as it sets foot on this earth of ours, it becomes splattered with blood and mire, it gives itself to a thousand men—but then it becomes a mother, enriches the earth, raises the spirit of the struggling God a bit higher. I despise romantic perceptions of the Idea. The Idea is like God himself—out of inconceivable crimes, out of infamies and stupidities, nevertheless it proceeds slowly, with toil, ascending this craggy earth of ours. Our duty is to try to find the rhythm of God's progression, and when we find it to adjust, as much as we can, the rhythms of our small and ephemeral life with his. Only thus may we mortals manage to achieve something immortal. Thus also may our life, our action and our thought achieve unity and character. We conquer circumstantial detail, we conquer boredom, we conquer the heart's narrowness, we feel that all men and all peoples—and further still, all plants, all animals—collaborate, and that we all ascend together, swept up by a mysterious and invisible Urge. Where are we going? No one knows. Don't ask, mount higher! Perhaps we are going nowhere, perhaps there is no one to pay us the rewarding wages of our lives. So much the better! For thus may we conquer the last, the greatest of all temptations—that of Hope. We fight because that is how we want it, without reward; we are not hired mercenaries. We sing even though we know that no ear exists to hear us; we toil though there is no employer to pay us our wages when night falls. We are despairing, serene, and free. This is true heroism, the highest achievement, it seems to me, of man." [14] God for Kazantzakis "was never created out of happiness, out of glory, out of comfort. Only out of shame, disgrace, and tears." "I would like," he wrote at that time, "to pass through the *experience* of Russia and afterwards to organize a method by which I may express the religious vision which possesses me."

His lifelong attraction to asceticism, to the lineaments of sainthood, made it impossible for him to partake personally in any action which might demean the purity of his thought, though in theory he understood clearly the necessity for such compromise. His dedication was not to men, but to Man, to the betterment of such material and spiritual conditions as might make the Overman of Nietzsche possible. He was dedicated not to that aspect of Nietzsche's *Übermensch* which has now taken on pejorative emphasis in the translation "Superman," but to the "Overman," to that person who struggles to overcome man's limitations, for man, says Zarathustra, "is a bridge and not an end," man must try to raise himself above the animals and the all-too-human, he must strain to overcome inertia

24

and cultural conditioning and to strive upward.

In *Toda Raba* Kazantzakis wrote: "That which interests me is not man, nor the earth, nor the heavens, but the flame which consumes man, earth, and sky. Russia does not interest me, but the flame which consumes Russia. Betterment of the fate of the masses or of the select, happiness, justice, virtue —these are vulgar bait which cannot hook me. One thing only moves me; I seek it everywhere and follow it with my eyes, with fear and joy: the crimson line which pierces and passes through men, as through a necklace of skulls. I don't love anything else, but only this crimson line; my singular happiness is to feel it splitting my skull into fragments as it pierces and penetrates. All other things seem to me ephemeral, stupidly philanthropic and vegetarian, unworthy of a soul which has freed itself of every hope. You know it well—my particular leader is not one of the three leaders of the human spirit, neither Faust, nor Hamlet, nor Don Quixote, but only Don Odysseus. It is on his ship that I came to the U.S.S.R. . . . He heard from the North, amid northernmost mist, a new Siren. The Slavic Siren. May we stand before her, without plugging up our ears, not bound to the mast, but going and coming throughout our ship, free men. We hear the beautiful song of the Siren, and keep our souls untouched. Motionless by the prow, Captain Odysseus shouts: 'Eh, comrades! Open your eyes, your ears, your nostrils, your mouth, your hands; open your brains; fill your entrails full!' " And it was finally in *The Odyssey: A Modern Sequel*, which he began to write the year after he had completed *The Saviors of God*, that the full form of his *Spiritual Exercises* was embodied, and by which he knew he must either live or die in the memory of man. Like all modern poets who have attempted epical works, whether as concentrated as T. S. Eliot's *The Waste Land* or Hart Crane's *The Bridge*, or as all-inclusive as Ezra Pound's *Cantos* or James Joyce's *Ulysses* or *Finnegans Wake*, Kazantzakis was forced to create his own ideology, since his age gave him none which he could accept as myth, religion, or symbol. He was fortunate to live in the one country in the world where ancient myths are still part of the blood and bone of its people. William Butler Yeats expended the greatest poetic talent of our century by delineating a system in his prose work, *A Vision*, which shows profound psychological and imaginative insight, and which should have been one of the great long poems of our time had it not been necessary for him to divert his creative powers into philosophical ordering. Dante had his Church and his Thomas Aquinas, and every long-visaged poet of our times must try to be Dante.[15]

The Saviors of God is the delineation of this flame which consumed the entire life and thought of Nikos Kazantzakis, brought him to many seeming paradoxes, made him anathema to the Greek Orthodox Church (which tried, unsuccessfully, to excommunicate him),[16] made him suspect for almost the entire duration of his life to parties of the middle, left, or right, and brought personal distress to the many persons who loved him yet felt they had never reached him, or that he had never given of himself to others. "You don't love man, you have no heart," a friend shouted at him, in Russia. "You don't care about the masses at all." "And I fell silent," Kazantzakis wrote, "because the pure, sentimental spirit of my friend could not understand this tigress, the hound of that God which I bear and which, like the Spartan boy who stole the fox, gnaws at my heart." "Every day I am more deeply confirmed," he wrote Mr. Prevelakis from Russia, "that something *inhuman* exists within me. Someone within me turns human desires and tendencies backward into something dark, cruel, unsated, despairing." From early youth, as he described it in *Zorba*, he had dreamed of withdrawing into the pure life of contemplation, and had even chosen the retreat: "Build an intellectual community and bury ourselves there; a dozen friends—musicians, poets, painters. . . . Work all day, meet only at night, eat, sing, read together, discuss the great problems of humanity, demolish the traditional answers. I had worked out the rules of the community already. I had even found the building in one of the passes of Mt. Hymettus, at St. John the Hunter." [17] For this reason he had been obsessed all his life long with those heroes who met the Tempter, resisted him, and transformed flesh into spirit. He had brooded long on the ultimate spiritual significance and martyrdom of Christ stripped of dogmatic and ceremonious ritual, had written a verse play, *Christ* (about 1921), a novel, *Christ Recrucified* (written in 1948, published in the United States as *The Greek Passion*, and later made into the French film *He Who Must Die*), and *The Last Temptation of Christ* (written in 1950–51). [18]

After he had finished *The Saviors of God* (1923) and had roamed restlessly throughout Germany, he left in January 1924 for Italy and was drawn, as by spiritual destiny, to the birthplace of the saint he most admired, to Assisi, where he remained for three months roaming the countryside where St. Francis

27

had once roamed, brooding on that saint whose identification with Christ had also brought him a deformation of the flesh: the stigmata. The spiritual tensions and antithetical struggles which had deformed the face of Kazantzakis in Vienna were never to leave him. Here in Assisi he met Johannes Joergensen, already famous for his life of St. Francis (which Kazantzakis was later to translate), and inquired into saintly causes. But it was not until 1953, after he had written *Buddha* and *The Saviors of God*, after four trips to Russia, and after three books on Christ, that he wrote a novelized life of St. Francis, entitled *The Poor Man of God*. In the preface he wrote: "Love, reverence, and admiration for the hero and great martyr possessed me when I wrote this legend, truer than truth. . . . I felt everywhere about me, as I was writing, his invisible presence, because for me St. Francis is the prototype of the militant man who with an unceasing and most difficult struggle achieves and carries out the highest duty of man, higher than morality or truth or beauty: to transubstantiate the matter which had been entrusted to him by God and to make it spirit."

As we were collaborating on the translation of his *Odyssey*, Nikos Kazantzakis told me many anecdotes, among them one about his life in Assisi, which I set down here as an example of a generosity of gesture that best symbolizes the amplitude of his soul. It was for qualities such as these that I most loved him. During his winter stay of three months in Assisi, he lived at the home of the Countess Enrichetta Pucci, who had turned her ancestral villa into a pension and now lived there with one maidservant. She was then seventy-seven years old, but

Kazantzakis thought he had never before seen such a lively, cheery, and charming old lady. She was fat, white-skinned, scrupulously clean, full of laughter, and open in her speech. Every night before he retired, they would huddle around clay braziers of burning coal, and Kazantzakis' soul softened as he listened to the eternal sufferings of man and the heroism of the soul as exemplified by this seventy-seven-year-old countess with "her superb mind, her lucid critical judgment, and her indomitable cheerfulness." At times she would fall silent and then soon after say to him, "Speak of anything." The stories he would tell her from his own life then would take on the shape of legend, and for the first time he realized what a wealth of material lay buried within him. Almost all these legends have now become part of his books, and one of his favorite expressions was one he put into the mouth of Odysseus when that god-slayer talked with Christ: "Tell me your myth that the whole world may turn to myth." [19] Sometimes of an afternoon she would send her maidservant to ask when she might visit him. The hour would be appointed, he would buy sweets and flowers, and then wait for her. After knocking, she would enter, vivacious and flushed; and he, too, would feel an extraordinary excitement. On leaving, she would be trembling slightly, and he could not doubt that between them there rose a refined and far-off erotic attraction. When he was to leave Assisi, she begged him to stay and offered to make him her heir, but he reluctantly and tactfully refused, and though she was close to eighty they agreed on a rendezvous for supper, to be kept exactly eight years later, to the day. He left, profoundly moved. Eight years later, as the appointed

29

day approached, Kazantzakis found himself in Spain, and remembering his date with the Countess, abandoned everything he was doing and hurriedly left for Italy, disdaining to find out first whether she was still alive. On the appointed hour he climbed with beating heart the steep ascent leading to her villa and knocked upon her door. It was opened by the same maidservant of eight years earlier, who politely informed him that the Countess was expecting him, that a supper of eggs was in readiness, but that due to her advanced old age it would be served in her boudoir. He found her enthroned in her bed, dressed in old and noble laces, presented her with the flowers and sweets he had brought, and then both fell weeping into each other's arms. After supper and a long, tender conversation, he left, never to see her again. A few months later she was dead.

From Italy he had written his wife: "I have a presentiment that all my religious endeavors will terminate in Russia." After his first trip to the Caucasus in 1919, he made his three other trips to Russia from mid-October through late January of 1925–1926, from late October through December of 1927, and from April 1928 to April 1929. During his last trip, he traveled alone in the cold depths of winter, from late January through March, first past Lapland, north to Murmansk, then east across the Urals into the freezing wastes of Siberia, past Perm, Omsk, and Iman to his destination, Vladivostok, on the far Pacific. He was profoundly impressed by the vast silences of the tundra (depicted with crystalline beauty in the last three books of *The Odyssey*), unmarked and untrammeled by the turmoils of man, where only fear and hunger reigned as the elemental emotions of survival, where the earth was stripped to nudity in a premonition of the silences of eternity. "Bitterness, savagery, love of the wilderness, contempt for hope, Silence, all these cross my breast," he wrote Mr. Prevelakis on his way to Murmansk. On February 18, 1929, he wrote from Vladivostok: "I have reached the ultimate point; I set up the mark of a difficult victory. Stubbornness, an inhuman love, contempt for men, faith and silence. Today it is my birthday; I am quiet, completely alone, and watch the Pacific Ocean before me filled with green frozen waves." On his return from Siberia to Moscow he wrote how happy he had been to keep his "mouth shut for weeks, unsoiled by any word," and he placed as the highest fruit of his experience "the great, fertile, divine Silence within me."

Some months before, from a country house on the outskirts of Moscow, he had written Mr. Prevelakis: "I am correcting my *Spiritual Exercises*, and I have added a small chapter entitled 'Silence.' It is a bomb which will explode all of *Spiritual Exercises*. But it will burst in the hearts of few men only." His revisions, however, were not fundamental, consisting mainly in polishing, refining, omitting, and in transposing some verses from one section to another. And although in fact he did "add" another chapter and entitled it "Silence," it was composed primarily of the last verses taken from "The Relationship Between Man and Nature" (with which the first, 1927, edition had closed) and preceded by the verses on Fire taken from the section entitled "The Vision." By thus transposing and combining old material and giving it the heading "The Silence," he did not so much construct a new bomb as add the fuse to an old one, particularly in the revised ending of the "incantation" with which the book closes.

In the first edition the beatitude read:

BLESSED be all those who hear, because they shall be saved, by fighting.

BLESSED be all those who are saved, because they free God, by creating.

BLESSED be all those who on their shoulders bear the Supreme Responsibility.

In the second edition, published in Athens in 1945, he regrouped some verses, numbered all of them, and printed the entire incantation in capital letters, omitting the verses I have just quoted, and substituting these:

7. BLESSED BE ALL THOSE WHO HEAR AND RUSH TO FREE YOU, LORD, AND WHO SAY: "ONLY YOU AND I EXIST."

8. BLESSED BE ALL THOSE WHO FREE YOU AND BE-COME UNITED WITH YOU, LORD, AND WHO SAY: "YOU AND I ARE ONE."

9. AND THRICE BLESSED BE THOSE WHO BEAR ON THEIR SHOULDERS AND DO NOT BUCKLE UNDER THIS GREAT, SUB-LIME, AND TERRIFYING SECRET:

THAT EVEN THIS ONE DOES NOT EXIST!

The inserted fuse which was to explode the bomb already in the text is, of course, the final annihilating statement. Kazantzakis repeated this beautifully in Book XVIII of *The Odyssey*, in the conversation between Odysseus, Prince Motherth (the representative type of Buddha), and Margaro, the famous courtesan.[20] When Odysseus asks Margaro for the distillation of all her experience in love, Margaro replies that she tells her lovers: "In all this wretched world, but you and I exist," and then, "Beloved, I feel at length that we two are but One." Odysseus replies that this is also the answer of the saint, but that there is a third synthesis: "Even this One, O Margaro, even this One is empty air."

These and similar statements have been interpreted, even by some of the most sensitive and informed readers and friends of Kazantzakis, to be an acceptance of "complete nihilism," and they incorrectly permit such definition to embrace the totality of his life. There can be no doubt that Kazantzakis fell into the deep well of nihilism, but this was true only of his late youth and middle age. He struggled his life long to free himself, one after another, from the many shackles with which man has bound himself. In 1936 he wrote Mr. Prevelakis: "The simplest plan which I found was this: Until 1923 I passed through Nationalism, all feeling and flame. . . . From 1923 to about 1933 I passed with the same feeling and flame the left-wing line-up, but I was never a Communist, as you know. . . . Now I am passing through the third—will it be my last? —stage: I call it Freedom. No shade accompanies me. Only my own, long, drawn out, deep black, ascending." "When I was a small boy," he wrote in *Zorba*, "it was necessary for me to fall, at some time or other, into a well. At school I was told the story of a boy who found, at the bottom of a well into which he had fallen, a most beautiful city. . . . I also wanted to find, in my turn, that beautiful city at the bottom of the well in our house. When I grew up I fell into the word 'eternity,' and afterwards into other words such as 'love,' 'hope,' 'country,' 'God.' Each time I thought that I had been saved, and continued on my way. But I had proceeded nowhere. I had simply changed words. And this is what I called Salvation. Now lately, for two whole years, I have been hanging on the rim of the word 'Buddha.' " [21]

It was Buddha who represented complete nihilism for Kazantzakis, the "last man" of Nietzsche, and he struggled to exorcise him from his own flesh and mind by trapping that "Enlightened One" in a verse drama and thus annihilating him, but in Vienna and in his subsequent life he suffered psychosomatically from the ravages of that vision. It is imperative to stress here that he finally rejected nihilism, or the *via negativa*, just as he rejected its counterpart, the hedonistic immersion in flesh. He rejected, that is, both Prince Motherth and Margaro, although if he had to choose between these two he would undoubtedly have preferred the seductress of flesh. All hangs on interpretation of the word "freedom," the keystone to Kazantzakis' philosophy. When Motherth hears Odysseus' dictum that "Even this One, O prince, even this One is empty air," he misinterprets, places the emphasis wrongly on nihilism, and exclaims:

> Freedom, herb of forgetfulness that blooms on
> cliffs,
> most precious antidote and balm of poisonous
> life,
> home-wrecking Liberty, well met! Your good
> health, worms!
> Seven well-hidden paths lead to salvation's
> grace

and I shall take the straitest road of black
    despair
and empty my full heart of sorrows, passions,
    joys.
Motherth, abjure your eyes, your ears, your
    nose, your tongue;
forswear, Motherth, all virtues, glories, deeds,
    and minds!
Forswear all earth's creations, they're but fan-
    tasies,
for we chase shadows, mounted on swift shad-
    owy steeds;
Death is a shadow, too, that hunts the shadow
    life;
O Motherth, shut your eyes, your ears, your
    nose, your mouth:
for even this one—do you hear?—this One is
    empty air! [22]

But in *Toda Raba*, Kazantzakis had related a Hindu
fable: "An Indian struggled for a long time against
the current which was pushing his bark toward the
cataract. When the great combatant finally understood that his every endeavor would be futile, he
crossed his oars and began to sing: 'Ah, may this
song become my life. I do not hope any more, I do
not fear any more, I am free.'" Earlier, Odysseus
had answered Motherth:

My son, I too watch Death before me night
    and day;
the proudest joy which now unites us here on
    earth

is that we've emptied both our hearts of gods
　　and hope;
yet you sink nerveless to the ground, for lone-
　　liness
has driven you wild, and freedom cleaves your
　　head in two.
But I hold Death like a black banner and march
　　on! [23]

On Kazantzakis' tombstone in Herakleion,
Crete, the following words have been engraved: "I
do not hope for anything. I do not fear anything.
I am free." [24]

Kazantzakis and his autobiographical hero Odysseus negate the negation. Having stripped themselves of every illusion (including that of Russia—
Kazantzakis in the Soviet itself, Odysseus in the destruction of his Ideal City), they looked full into
the eyes of annihilation, faced the final seduction
of "rotten-thighed Hope" [25]—hope of personal immortality, or of God as a fixed, predetermined and
final end—then embraced the Void, the Silence.
"What freedom?" Odysseus cries. And answers:
"To stare into the black eyes of the Abyss/with gal-
lantry and joy as on one's native land." [26] Among
Kazantzakis' posthumous papers Mr. Prevelakis
found this note written in his own hand: "Toward
the end Odysseus' religion became unshakable, so
that no idea or act could any longer tear it down—
because, indeed, it was based on the Void; neither
God, nor hope, nor fear, nor eternity. Every moment was itself deathless, and he had no need of
any other deathlessness. He lived every moment
intensely, with quality." Kazantzakis' attitude to-

ward life has been called "heroic pessimism" and "Dionysian nihilism," but again the emphasis has been misapplied, for what are here the adjectival modifiers were in fact the essential substances of his life and thought. "I am becoming more and more *amoral*, more and more *anidéal*," he wrote Mr. Prevelakis, "yet not with the negative but with the positive and profound content of these words, for they are negative only to barren, unfeeling, cold souls." In Kazantzakis' own life, and in that of his imaginary hero, a period of denial did indeed follow any cataclysm. But from that Nietzsche who pronounced the death of the dogmatic Christian God, Kazantzakis learned, as Zarathustra said, that "only that life is worth living which develops the strength and the integrity to withstand the unavoidable sufferings and misfortunes of existence without flying into an imaginary world"; and throughout *The Saviors of God* will be found the tonality, the imprint, the style, and the structure of *Thus Spake Zarathustra*, which together with *The Birth of Tragedy* Kazantzakis had translated into Greek. From Bergson he learned that all of nature, all of the pluriverse, all of life was the expression of an evolutionary drive, an *élan vital*, an inconceivable energy which ceaselessly renews itself, a continual creativity, a leap upward, not toward a fixed, predetermined, final end, but within a teleology immanent in the life force itself, which was creating its own perfectability as it evolved eternally. This creativity toward a perfectability never reached but always postulated, this agonized transmutation of matter into spirit, is what Kazantzakis meant by God. "Bergson," he wrote, "disburdened me from unresolvable agonies which tormented my early youth. Nietzsche enriched me with new agonies and taught me to transubstantiate unhappiness, sorrow, and uncertainty into pride. And Zorba? He taught me to love life and not to fear death."

Bergson and Nietzsche must stand as the two main streams of Kazantzakis' philosophical thought; [27] but on this current sailed the many Saviors of God who served as the bodyguards of his spirit and who helped him conclude that God is not a teleology, not an entelechy, not a predetermined Father, Son, or Holy Ghost who aids man in the salvation of his soul; and that Man himself is only one manifestation in the long, evolutionary, upward progress of mysterious and vital forces—perhaps the finest yet evolved in the history of earth, the most capable of spiritual refinement, yet certainly not the last or the best possible; and that it is Man in his struggle with the material elements of his nature who might be the Savior of God and bring Him to more and more spiritual essence. Kazantzakis wrote a group of about twenty poems in *terza rima* dedicated to these Saviors of God, whom he called the Bodyguards of the Odyssey. Among these are Moses, Buddha, Alexander the Great, Christ, Mohammed, Genghis Khan, Dante, Leonardo da Vinci, St. Theresa, Don Quixote, El Greco, Shakespeare, Nietzsche, Lenin. Kazantzakis told me that these bodyguards often appeared in his life in conflicting dualities of thesis and antithesis, as in Christ-Zorba, Buddha-Lenin; but there can be no doubt that in Odysseus he found a character ample enough to contain the dualities without either resolving them into harmonious sterility or suffering an explosion of irreconcilable forces, a "man of many turns" who could keep both extremities in a vital and fluid interchange, as the searing and luminous electrical current that passes between the positive and negative poles of electricity and becomes more violent, though seemingly more inactive, as the two poles approach each other in an illusion of harmonious entity, the still center in the whirling hub of a wheel. Both Kazantzakis and Odysseus were "men of mixed motives in a constant state of ethical tension." [23]

No religious dogma, no political ideology may claim Nikos Kazantzakis. His works will always be a heresy to any political or religious faith which exists today or which may be formulated in the future, for in the heart of his *Spiritual Exercises* lies a bomb timed to explode all visions which are betrayed into the petrifaction of ritual, constitution, or dogma. His works are not solid land where a pilgrim might stake his claim, but the ephemeral stopping stations of a moment where the traveler might catch his breath before he abandons them also, and again strives upward on the steep ascent, leaving behind him the bloody trail of his endeavor. The fate of all heresies is to solidify, in the petrifaction of time, into stable and comforting orthodoxies. It would be the deepest happiness of Nikos Kazantzakis to know that those whom his works have helped to mount a step higher in the evolutionary growth of the spirit have smashed the Tablets of his Law, denied him, betrayed him, and struggled to surpass him, to mount higher on their own naked wings. His parting words to these would be those he put into the mouth of Odysseus when that bold Death Archer said farewell to one of his departing disciples:

Blessed be the bold, audacious daring of your
    youth!
Steady your knees, my friend, don't let my
    blessing throw you:
now may that winnower God, who scatters age
    like chaff,
grant you the power to cast the disk of earth
    much further.
Dear God, how many foaming seas, how much
    green earth,
how many multicolored birds and sweet desires
I'll never have time enough to taste before I
    die
like a poor beggar with outstretched and greedy
    palms!
May you reach that far land I've aimed at since
    my birth
and, if you can, load my large flowering tree
    with fruit.[29]

KIMON FRIAR
New York
September 1959

Prologue

W E COME *from a dark abyss, we end in a dark abyss, and we call the luminous interval life.* ☼ *As soon as we are born the return begins, at once the setting forth and the coming back; we die in every moment.* ☼ *Because of this many have cried out: The goal of life is death!* ☼ *But as soon as we are born we begin the struggle to create, to compose, to turn matter into life; we are born in every moment.* ☼ *Because of this many have cried out: The goal of ephemeral life is immortality!* ☼ *In the temporary living organism these two streams collide: (a) the ascent toward composition, toward life, toward immortality; (b) the descent toward decomposition, toward matter, toward death.* ☼ *Both streams well up*

from the depths of primordial essence. Life star-
tles us at first; it seems somewhat beyond the law,
somewhat contrary to nature, somewhat like a
transitory counteraction to the dark eternal foun-
tains; but deeper down we feel that Life is itself
without beginning, an indestructible force of the
Universe. ✸ *Otherwise, from where did that su-*
perhuman strength come which hurls us from the
unborn to the born and gives us—plants, animals,
men—courage for the struggle? But both oppos-
ing forces are holy. ✸ *It is our duty, therefore, to*
grasp that vision which can embrace and harmo-
nize these two enormous, timeless, and indestruct-
ible forces, and with this vision to modulate our
thinking and our action.

The
Preparation

First Duty

WITH CLARITY *and quiet, I look upon the world and say: All that I see, hear, taste, smell, and touch are the creations of my mind.*

✿ *2. The sun comes up and the sun goes down in my skull. Out of one of my temples the sun rises, and into the other the sun sets.*

✿ *3. The stars shine in my brain; ideas, men, animals browse in my temporal head; songs and weeping fill the twisted shells of my ears and storm the air for a moment.*

✿ *4. My brain blots out, and all, the heavens and the earth, vanish.*

✿ *5. The mind shouts: "Only I exist!*

✿ *6. "Deep in my subterranean cells my five*

47

senses labor; they weave and unweave space and time, joy and sorrow, matter and spirit.

7. "All swirl about me like a river, dancing and whirling; faces tumble like water, and chaos howls.

⚙ 8. "But I, the Mind, continue to ascend patiently, manfully, sober in the vertigo. That I may not stumble and fall, I erect landmarks over this vertigo; I sling bridges, open roads, and build over the abyss.

⚙ 9. "Struggling slowly, I move among the phenomena which I create, I distinguish between them for my convenience, I unite them with laws and yoke them to my heavy practical needs.

⚙ 10. "I impose order on disorder and give a face—my face—to chaos.

⚙ 11. "I do not know whether behind appearances there lives and moves a secret essence superior to me. Nor do I ask; I do not care. I create phenomena in swarms, and paint with a full palette a gigantic and gaudy curtain before the abyss. Do not say, 'Draw the curtain that I may see the painting.' The curtain IS the painting.

⚙ 12. "This kingdom is my child, a transitory, a human work. But it's a solid work, nothing more solid exists, and only within its boundaries can I remain fruitful, happy, and at work.

⚙ 13. "I am the worker of the abyss. I am the spectator of the abyss. I am both theory and practice. I am the law. Nothing beyond me exists."

To SEE and accept the boundaries of the human mind without vain rebellion, and in these severe limitations to work ceaselessly without protest—this is where man's first duty lies.

⚙ 15. Build over the unsteady abyss, with manliness and austerity, the fully round and luminous arena of the mind where you may thresh and winnow the universe like a lord of the land.

⚙ 16. Distinguish clearly these bitter yet fertile human truths, flesh of our flesh, and admit them heroically: (a) the mind of man can perceive appearances only, and never the essence of things; (b) and not all appearances but only the appearances of matter; (c) and more narrowly still: not even these appearances of matter, but only relationships between them; (d) and these relationships are not real and independent of man, for even these are his creations; (e) and they are not the only ones humanly possible, but simply the most convenient for his practical and perceptive needs.

⚙ 17. Within these limitations the mind is the legal and absolute monarch. No other power reigns within its kingdom.

⚙ 18. I recognize these limitations, I accept them with resignation, bravery, and love, and I struggle at ease in their enclosure, as though I were free.

⚙ 19. I subdue matter and force it to become

49

my mind's good medium. I rejoice in plants, in animals, in man and in gods, as though they were my children. I feel all the universe nestling about me and following me as though it were my own body.

❁ 20. *In sudden dreadful moments a thought flashes through me: "This is all a cruel and futile game, without beginning, without end, without meaning." But again I yoke myself swiftly to the wheels of necessity, and all the universe begins to revolve around me once more.*

❁ 21. *Discipline is the highest of all virtues. Only so may strength and desire be counterbalanced and the endeavors of man bear fruit.*

❁ 22. *This is how, with clarity and austerity, you may determine the omnipotence of the mind amid appearances and the incapacity of the mind beyond appearances—before you set out for salvation. You may not otherwise be saved.*

❁

❁

I WILL NOT *accept boundaries; appearances cannot contain me; I choke! To bleed in this agony, and to live it profoundly, is the second duty.*

❁ 2. *The mind is patient and adjusts itself, it*

likes to play; but the heart grows savage and will not condescend to play; it stifles and rushes to tear apart the nets of necessity.

⚙ 3. What is the value of subduing the earth, the waters, the air, of conquering space and time, of understanding what laws govern the mirages that rise from the burning deserts of the mind, their appearance and reappearance?

⚙ 4. I have one longing only: to grasp what is hidden behind appearances, to ferret out that mystery which brings me to birth and then kills me, to discover if behind the visible and unceasing stream of the world an invisible and immutable presence is hiding.

⚙ 5. If the mind cannot, if it was not made to attempt the heroic and desperate breach beyond frontiers, then if only the heart could!

⚙ 6. Beyond! Beyond! Beyond! Beyond man I seek the invisible whip which strikes him and drives him into the struggle. I lie in ambush to find out what primordial face struggles beyond animals to imprint itself on the fleeting flesh by creating, smashing, and remolding innumerable masks. I struggle to make out beyond plants the first stumbling steps of the Invisible in the mud.

⚙ 7. A command rings out within me: "Dig! What do you see?"

"Men and birds, water and stones."

"Dig deeper! What do you see?"

"Ideas and dreams, fantasies and lightning flashes!"

"Dig deeper! What do you see?"

"I see nothing! A mute Night, as thick as death. It must be death."

"Dig deeper!"

"Ah! I cannot penetrate the dark partition! I hear voices and weeping. I hear the flutter of wings on the other shore."

"Don't weep! Don't weep! They are not on the other shore. The voices, the weeping, and the wings are your own heart."

⚙ 8. Beyond the mind, on the edge of the heart's holy precipice, I proceed, trembling. One foot grips the secure soil, the other gropes in the darkness above the abyss.

⚙ 9. Behind all appearances, I divine a struggling essence. I want to merge with it.

⚙ 10. I feel that behind appearances this struggling essence is also striving to merge with my heart. But the body stands between us and separates us. The mind stands between us and separates us.

⚙ 11. What is my duty? To shatter the body, to rush and merge with the Invisible. To let the mind fall silent that I may hear the Invisible calling.

⚙ 12. I walk on the rim of the abyss, and I tremble. Two voices contend within me.

⚙ 13. The mind: "Why waste ourselves by pursuing the impossible? Within the holy enclosure of our five senses it is our duty to acknowledge the limitations of man."

✸ 14. But another voice within me—call it the Sixth Power, call it the heart—resists and shouts: "No! No! Never acknowledge the limitations of man. Smash all boundaries! Deny whatever your eyes see. Die every moment, but say: 'Death does not exist.'"

✸ 15. The mind: "My eye is without hope or illusion and gazes on all things clearly. Life is a game, a performance given by the five actors of my body.

✸ 16. "I look on avidly, with inexpressible curiosity, but I am not like the naïve peasant to believe what I see, clambering on the stage to meddle with the blood-drenched comedy.

✸ 17. "I am the wonder-working fakir who sits unmoving at the crossroads of the senses and watches the world being born and destroyed, watches the mob as it surges and shouts in the multicolored paths of vanity.

✸ 18. "Heart, naïve heart, become serene, and surrender!"

✸ 19. But the heart leaps up and shouts: "I am the peasant who jumps on the stage to meddle with the course of the world!"

✸ 20. I don't keep checks and balances, I don't seek to adjust myself. I follow the deep throbbing of my heart.

✸ 21. I ask and ask again, beating on chaos: "Who plants us on this earth without asking our permission? Who uproots us from this earth without asking our permission?"

☼ 22. I am a weak, ephemeral creature made of mud and dream. But I feel all the powers of the universe whirling within me.

☼ 23. Before they crush me, I want to open my eyes for a moment and to see them. I set my life no other purpose.

☼ 24. I want to find a single justification that I may live and bear this dreadful daily spectacle of disease, of ugliness, of injustice, of death.

☼ 25. I once set out from a dark point, the Womb, and now I proceed to another dark point, the Tomb. A power hurls me out of the dark pit and another power drags me irrevocably toward the dark pit.

☼ 26. I am not like the condemned man whose mind has been deadened with drink. Stone sober, with a clear head, I stride along a narrow path between two cliffs.

☼ 27. And I strive to discover how to signal my companions before I die, how to give them a hand, how to spell out for them in time one complete word at least, to tell them what I think this procession is, and toward what we go. And how necessary it is for all of us together to put our steps and hearts in harmony.

☼ 28. To say in time a simple word to my companions, a password, like conspirators.

☼ 29. Yes, the purpose of Earth is not life, it is not man. Earth has existed without these, and it will live on without them. They are but the ephemeral sparks of its violent whirling.

❁ 30. Let us unite, let us hold each other tightly, let us merge our hearts, let us create—so long as the warmth of this earth endures, so long as no earthquakes, cataclysms, icebergs or comets come to destroy us—let us create for Earth a brain and a heart, let us give a human meaning to the superhuman struggle.

❁ 31. This anguish is our second duty.

❁

Third Duty

❁

THE MIND adjusts itself. It wants to fill its dungeon, the skull, with great works, to engrave on the walls heroic mottoes, to paint on its shackles the wings of freedom.

❁ 2. The heart cannot adjust itself. Hands beat on the wall outside its dungeon, it listens to erotic cries that fill the air. Then, swollen with hope, the heart responds by rattling its chains; for a brief moment it believes that its chains have turned to wings.

❁ 3. But swiftly the heart falls wounded again, it loses all hope, and is gripped once more by the Great Fear.

❁ 4. The moment is ripe: leave the heart and

the mind behind you, go forward, take the third step.

☼ *5. Free yourself from the simple compla-cency of the mind that thinks to put all things in order and hopes to subdue phenomena. Free yourself from the terror of the heart that seeks and hopes to find the essence of things.*

☼ *6. Conquer the last, the greatest temptation of all: Hope. This is the third duty.*

☼ *7. We fight because we like fighting, we sing even though there is no ear to hear us. We work even though there is no master to pay us our wages when night falls. We do not work for others, we are the masters. This vineyard of earth is ours, our own flesh and blood.*

☼ *8. We cultivate and prune it, we gather its grapes and tread them, we drink its wine, we sing and we weep, ideas and visions rise in our heads.*

☼ *9. In what season of the vineyard has it fallen your lot to work? In the digging? In the vintage? In the feasting? All these are one.*

☼ *10. I dig and rejoice in the grapes' entire cycle. I sing as I thirst and toil, drunk with the wine to come.*

☼ *11. I hold the brimming wineglass and relive the toils of my grandfathers and great-grandfath-ers. The sweat of my labor runs down like a foun-tain from my tall, intoxicated brow.*

☼ *12. I am a sack filled with meat and bones,*

blood, sweat, and tears, desires and visions.

☀ 13. *I revolve for a moment in air, I breathe, my heart beats, my mind glows, and suddenly the earth opens, and I vanish.*

☀ 14. *In my ephemeral backbone the two eternal streams rise and fall. In my vitals a man and woman embrace. They love and hate each other, they fight.*

☀ 15. *The man is smothering, and he cries out: "I am the shuttle that longs to tear apart the warp and woof, to leap out of the loom of necessity.*

☀ 16. "To go beyond the law, to smash bodies, to conquer death. I am the Seed!"

☀ 17. *And the other, profound voice, alluring and womanly, replies with serenity and surety: "I sit cross-legged on the ground and spread my roots deep under the tombs. Motionless, I receive the seed and nourish it. I am all milk and necessity.*

☀ 18. "And I long to turn back, to descend into the beast, to descend even lower, into the tree, within the roots and the soil, and there never to move.*

☀ 19. "I hold back the Spirit to enslave it, I won't let it escape, for I hate the flame which rises ever upward. I am the Womb!"

☀ 20. *And I listen to the two voices; they are both mine; I rejoice in them and deny neither* one. My heart is a dance of the five senses; my heart is a counterdance in denial of the five senses.

❀ 21. Innumerable powers, visible and invisible, rejoice and follow me when, fighting against the almighty current, I ascend with agony.

❀ 22. Innumerable powers, visible and invisible, are relieved and grow calm again when I descend and return to earth.

❀ 23. My heart streams on. I do not seek the beginning and the end of the world. I follow my heart's dread rhythm and plod on!

❀ 24. Say farewell to all things at every moment. Fix your eyes slowly, passionately, on all things and say: "Never again!"

❀ 25. Look about you: All these bodies that you see shall rot. There is no salvation.

❀ 26. Look at them well: They live, work, love, hope. Look again: Nothing exists!

❀ 27. The generations of man rise from the earth and fall into the earth again.

❀ 28. The endeavors and virtues of man accumulate, increase, and mount to the sky.

❀ 29. Where are we going? Do not ask! Ascend, descend. There is no beginning and no end. Only this present moment exists, full of bitterness, full of sweetness, and I rejoice in it all.

❀ 30. Life is good and death is good; the earth is round and firm in the experienced palms of my hands like the breast of a woman.

❀ 31. I surrender myself to everything. I love,

I feel pain, I struggle. The world seems to me wider than the mind, my heart a dark and almighty mystery.

☼ *32. If you can, Spirit, rise up over the roaring waves and take in all the sea with an encircling glance. Hold the mind fast, don't let it be shaken. Then plunge suddenly into the waves once more and continue the struggle.*

☼ *33. Our body is a ship that sails on deep blue waters. What is our goal? To be shipwrecked!*

☼ *34. Because the Atlantic is a cataract, the new Earth exists only in the heart of man, and suddenly, in a silent whirlpool, you will sink into the cataract of death, you and the whole world's galleon.*

☼ *35. Without hope, but with bravery, it is your duty to set your prow calmly toward the abyss. And to say: "Nothing exists!"*

☼ *36. Nothing exists! Neither life nor death. I watch mind and matter hunting each other like two nonexistent erotic phantasms—merging, begetting, disappearing—and I say: "This is what I want!"*

☼ *37. I know now: I do not hope for anything. I do not fear anything, I have freed myself from both the mind and the heart, I have mounted much higher, I am free. This is what I want. I want nothing more. I have been seeking freedom.*

The March

BUT SUDDENLY *a convulsive cry tears through me: "Help me!" Who calls?*

※ *2. Gather your strength and listen; the whole heart of man is a single outcry. Lean against your breast to hear it; someone is struggling and shouting within you.*

※ *3. It is your duty every moment, day and night, in joy or in sorrow, amid all daily necessities, to discern this Cry with vehemence or restraint, according to your nature, with laughter or with weeping, in action or in thought, striving to find out who is imperiled and cries out.*

※ *4. And how we may all be mobilized together to free him.*

※ *5. Amidst our greatest happiness someone*

within us cries out: "I am in pain! I want to escape your happiness! I am stifling!"

✤ 6. Amidst our deepest despair someone within us cries out: "I do not despair! I fight on! I grasp at your head, I unsheathe myself from your body, I detach myself from the earth, I cannot be contained in brains, in names, in deeds!"

✤ 7. Out of our most ample virtue someone rises up in despair and cries out: "Virtue is narrow, I cannot breathe! Paradise is small and cannot contain me! Your God resembles a man, I do not want him!"

✤ 8. I hear the savage cry, and I shudder. The agony that ascends within me composes itself, for the first time, into an integral human voice; it turns full face toward me and calls me clearly, with my own name, with the name of my father and my race.

✤ 9. This is the moment of greatest crisis. This is the signal for the March to begin. If you do not hear this Cry tearing at your entrails, do not set out.

✤ 10. Continue, with patience and submission, your sacred military service in the first, second, and third rank of preparation.

✤ 11. And listen: In sleep, in an act of love or of creation, in a proud and disinterested act of yours, or in a profound despairing silence, you may suddenly hear the Cry and set forth.

✤ 12. Until that moment my heart streams on,

64

it rises and falls with the Universe. But when I hear the Cry, my emotions and the Universe are divided into two camps.

※ 13. Someone within me is in danger, he raises his hands and shouts: "Save me!" Someone within me climbs, stumbles, and shouts: "Help me!"

※ 14. Which of the two eternal roads shall I choose? Suddenly I know that my whole life hangs on this decision—the life of the entire Universe.

※ 15. Of the two, I choose the ascending path. Why? For no intelligible reason, without any certainty; I know how ineffectual the mind and all the small certainties of man can be in this moment of crisis.

※ 16. I choose the ascending path because my heart drives me toward it. "Upward! Upward! Upward!" my heart shouts, and I follow it trustingly.

※ 17. I feel this is what the dread primordial cry asks of me. I leap to its side. I cast in my lot with its own.

※ 18. Someone within me is struggling to lift a great weight, to cast off the mind and flesh by overcoming habit, laziness, necessity.

※ 19. I do not know from where he comes or where he goes. I clutch at his onward march in my ephemeral breast, I listen to his panting struggle, I shudder when I touch him.

✹ 20. *Who is he? I prick up my ears. I set up various signs, I sniff the air. I ascend, groping upwards, panting and struggling. The dread and mystical March begins.*

First Step

THE EGO

I AM NOT *good, I am not innocent, I am not serene. My happiness and unhappiness are both unbearable; I am full of inarticulate voices and darknesses; I wallow, all blood and tears, in this warm trough of my flesh.*

✹ 2. *I am afraid to talk. I adorn myself with false wings; I shout, I sing and I weep to drown out the inexorable cry of my heart.*

✹ 3. *I am not the light, I am the night; but a flame stabs through my entrails and consumes me. I am the night devoured by light.*

✹ 4. *Imperiled, moaning and staggering in darkness, I strive to shake myself free from sleep and to stand erect for a while, for as long as I can bear.*

✹ 5. *A small but undaunted breath within me*

66

struggles desperately to vanquish happiness, weariness, death.

❀ 6. I put my body through its paces like a war horse; I keep it lean, sturdy, prepared. I harden it and I pity it. I have no other steed.

❀ 7. I keep my brain wide awake, lucid, unmerciful. I unleash it to battle relentlessly so that, all light, it may devour the darkness of the flesh. I have no other workshop where I may transform darkness into light.

❀ 8. I keep my heart flaming, courageous, restless. I feel in my heart all commotions and all contradictions, the joys and sorrows of life. But I struggle to subdue them to a rhythm superior to that of the mind, harsher than that of my heart—to the ascending rhythm of the Universe.

❀ 9. The Cry within me is a call to arms. It shouts: "I, the Cry, am the Lord your God! I am not an asylum. I am not hope and a home. I am not the Father nor the Son nor the Holy Ghost. I am your General!

❀ 10. "You are not my slave, nor a plaything in my hands. You are not my friend, you are not my child. You are my comrade-in-arms!

❀ 11. "Hold courageously the passes which I entrusted to you; do not betray them. You are in duty bound, and you may act heroically by remaining at your own battle station.

❀ 12. "Love danger. What is most difficult? That is what I want! Which road should you *take? The most craggy ascent! It is the one I also take: follow me!*

☼ 13. "Learn to obey. Only he who obeys a rhythm superior to his own is free.

☼ 14. "Learn to command. Only he who can give commands may represent me here on earth.

☼ 15. "Love responsibility. Say: 'It is my duty, and mine alone, to save the earth. If it is not saved, then I alone am to blame.'

☼ 16. "Love each man according to his contribution in the struggle. Do not seek friends; seek comrades-in-arms.

☼ 17. "Be always restless, unsatisfied, unconforming. Whenever a habit becomes convenient, smash it! The greatest sin of all is satisfaction.

☼ 18. "Where are we going? Shall we ever win? What is the purpose of all this fighting? Be silent! Soldiers never question!"

☼ 19. I stoop and listen to this war cry within me. I begin to discern the face of my Leader, to distinguish his voice, to accept harsh commands with joy and terror.

☼ 20. Yes, yes, I am NOT nothing! A vaporous phosphorescence on a damp meadow, a miserable worm that crawls and loves, that shouts and talks about wings for an hour or two until his mouth is blocked with earth. The dark powers give no other answer.

☼ 21. But within me a deathless Cry, superior to me, continues to shout. For whether I want to or not, I am also, without doubt, a part of the visible and the invisible Universe. We are one. The powers which labor within me, the powers which goad me on to live, the powers which goad me on to die are, without doubt, its own powers also.

✻ 22. I am not a suspended, rootless thing in the world. I am earth of its earth and breath of its breath.

✻ 23. I am not alone in my fear, nor alone in my hope, nor alone in my shouting. A tremendous host, an onrush of the Universe fears, hopes, and shouts with me.

✻ 24. I am an improvised bridge, and when Someone passes over me, I crumble away behind Him. A Combatant passes through me, eats my flesh and brain to open up roads, to free himself from me at last. It is not I but He who shouts.

Second Step

THE RACE

THE CRY is not yours. It is not you talking, but innumerable ancestors talking with your mouth. It is not you who desire, but innumerable generations of descendants longing with your heart.

✻ 2. Your dead do not lie in the ground. They have become birds, trees, air. You sit under their shade, you are nourished by their flesh, you inhale their breathing. They have become ideas and passions, they determine your will and your actions.

✻ 3. Future generations do not move far from you in an uncertain time. They live, desire, and act in your loins and your heart.

✻ 4. In this lightning moment when you walk the earth, your first duty, by enlarging your ego, is to live through the endless march, both visible and invisible, of your own being.

✻ 5. You are not one; you are a body of troops. One of your faces lights up for a moment under the sun. Then suddenly it vanishes, and another, a younger one, lights up behind you.

✻ 6. The race of men from which you come is the huge body of the past, the present, and the future. It is the face itself; you are a passing expression. You are the shadow; it is the meat.

✻ 7. You are not free. Myriad invisible hands hold your hands and direct them. When you rise in anger, a great-grandfather froths at your mouth; when you make love, an ancestral caveman growls with lust; when you sleep, tombs open in your memory till your skull brims with ghosts.

✻ 8. Your skull is a pit of blood round which the shades of the dead gather in myriad flocks to drink of you and be revived.

70

☼ 9. "Do not die that we may not die," the dead cry out within you. "We had no time to enjoy the women we desired; be in time, sleep with them! We had no time to turn our thoughts into deeds; turn them into deeds! We had no time to grasp and to crystallize the face of our hope; make it firm!

☼ 10. "Finish our work! Finish our work! All day and all night we come and go through your body, and we cry out. No, we have not gone, we have not detached ourselves from you, we have not descended into the earth. Deep in your entrails we continue the struggle. Deliver us!"

IT IS NOT enough to hear the tumult of ancestors within you. It is not enough to feel them battling at the threshold of your mind. All rush to clutch your warm brain and to climb once more into the light of day.

☼ 12. But you must choose with care whom to hurl down again into the chasms of your blood, and whom you shall permit to mount once more into the light and the earth.

☼ 13. Do not pity them. Keep vigil over the bottomless gulf of your heart, and choose. You shall say: "This shade is humble, dark, like a beast: send him away! This one is silent and flaming, more living than I: let him drink all my blood!"

☼ 14. Enlighten the dark blood of your ancestors, shape their cries into speech, purify their will, widen their narrow, unmerciful brows. This is your second duty.

☼ 15. For you are not only a slave. As soon as you were born, a new possibility was born with you, a free heartbeat stormed through the great sunless heart of your race.

☼ 16. Whether you would or not, you brought a new rhythm, a new desire, a new idea, a fresh sorrow. Whether you would or not, you enriched your ancestral body.

☼ 17. Where are you going? How shall you confront life and death, virtue and fear? All the race takes refuge in your breast; it asks questions there and lies waiting in agony.

☼ 18. You have a great responsibility. You do not govern now only your own small, insignificant existence. You are a throw of the dice on which, for a moment, the entire fate of your race is gambled.

☼ 19. Everything you do reverberates throughout a thousand destinies. As you walk, you cut open and create that river bed into which the stream of your descendants shall enter and flow.

☼ 20. When you shake with fear, your terror branches out into innumerable generations, and you degrade innumerable souls before and behind you. When you rise to a valorous deed, all of your race rises with you and turns valorous.

☼ 21. "I am not alone! I am not alone!" Let this vision inflame you at every moment.

☼　22. *You are not a miserable and momentary body; behind your fleeting mask of clay, a thousand-year-old face lies in ambush. Your passions and your thoughts are older than your heart or brain.*

☼　23. *Your invisible body is your dread ancestors and your unborn descendants. Your visible body is the living men, women, and children of your own race.*

☼　24. *Only he has been freed from the inferno of his ego who feels deep pangs of hunger when a child of his race has nothing to eat, who feels his heart throbbing with joy when a man and a woman of his race embrace and kiss one another.*

☼　25. *All these are limbs of your larger, visible body. You suffer and rejoice, scattered to the ends of the earth in a thousand bodies, blood of your blood.*

☼　26. *Fight on behalf of your larger body just as you fight on behalf of your smaller body. Fight that all of your bodies may become strong, lean, prepared, that their minds may become enlightened, that their flaming, manly, and restless hearts may throb.*

☼　27. *How can you become strong, enlightened, manly, if all these virtues do not storm throughout your entire larger body? How can you be saved unless all your blood is saved? If but one of your race is lost, he drags you down with him to destruction. A limb of your body and your mind rots.*

☸ 28. Be deeply alive to this identity, not as theory, but as flesh and blood.

☸ 29. You are a leaf on the great tree of your race. Feel the earth mounting from dark roots and spreading out into branches and leaves.

☸ 30. What is your goal? To struggle and to cling firmly to a branch, either as a leaf or flower or fruit, so that within you the entire tree may move and breathe and be renewed.

YOUR FIRST duty, in completing your service to your race, is to feel within you all your ancestors. Your second duty is to throw light on their onrush and to continue their work. Your third duty is to pass on to your son the great mandate to surpass you.

☸ 32. Agony within you! Someone is fighting to escape you, to tear himself away from your flesh, to be freed of you. A seed in your loins, a seed in your brains, does not want to remain with you any more. It cannot be contained in your entrails any longer; it fights for freedom.

☸ 33. "Father, I cannot be contained in your heart! I want to smash it and pass through! Father, I hate your body, I am ashamed to be glued to you, I want to leave you.

☸ 34. "You are nothing now but a sluggish horse, your feet can no longer follow the rhythm of my heart. I am in haste, Father. I shall dismount, I shall mount another body, and I shall leave you on the road."

🌼 35. And you, the father, rejoice to hear the contemptuous voice of your child. "All, all for my son!" you shout. "I am nothing. I am the Ape, he is the Man. I am the Man, he is the Son of Man!"

🌼 36. A power greater than you passes through you, smashing your body and mind, shouting: "Gamble the present and all things certain, gamble them for the future and all things uncertain!

🌼 37. "Hold nothing in reserve. I love danger! We may be lost, we may be saved. Do not ask. Place the whole world in the hands of danger every single moment. I, the seed of the unborn, eat at the entrails of your race, and I shout!"

Third Step

MANKIND

IT IS NOT you talking. Nor is it your race only which shouts within you, for all the innumerable races of mankind shout and rush within you: white, yellow, black.

☸   2. Free yourself from race also; fight to live through the whole struggle of man. See how he has detached himself from the animal, how he struggles to stand upright, to co-ordinate his inarticulate cries, to feed the flame between his hearthstones, to feed his mind amid the bones of his skull.

☸   3. Let pity overwhelm you for this creature who one morning detached himself from the ape, naked, defenseless, without teeth or horns, with only a spark of fire in his soft skull.

☸   4. He does not know from where he comes or where he goes. But by loving, toiling, and killing, he wants to conquer the earth.

☸   5. Look upon men and pity them. Look at yourself amid all men and pity yourself. In the obscure dusk of life we touch and fumble at each other, we ask questions, we listen, we shout for help.

☸   6. We run. We know that we are running to die, but we cannot stop. We run.

☸   7. We carry a torch and run. Our faces light up for a moment, but hurriedly we surrender the torch to our son, and then suddenly vanish and descend into Hades.

☸   8. The mother looks ahead, toward her daughter; the daughter in turn looks ahead, beyond the body of her husband, toward her son—

this is how the Invisible proceeds on earth.

❁ 9. We all look directly before us, ruthlessly, driven by dark, enormous, infallible powers behind us.

❁ 10. Rise above the improvised bastion of your body, look at the centuries behind you. What do you see? Hairy, blood-splattered beasts rising in tumult out of the mud. Hairy, blood-splattered beasts descending in tumult from the mountain summits.

❁ 11. The two bellowing armies meet like a man and a woman and become a lump of mud, blood, and brain.

❁ 12. Behold: multitudes ascend like grass out of the soil and fall into the soil again, fertile manure for future offspring. And the earth grows fat from the ashes, the blood, and the brains of man.

❁ 13. Numbers without end vanish in midjourney; they are born, but they die barren. Huge pits suddenly gape in the darkness, multitudes tumble and fall, disorderly commands are heard in confused clamor, and the human herd stampedes and scatters.

❁ 14. Below and about us and within the abyss of our hearts we suddenly become aware of blind, heartless, brainless, ravenous powers.

❁ 15. We sail on a storm-tossed sea, and in a yellow lightning flash we feel we've entrusted our wealth, our children, and our gods to an eggshell.

✿   16. *The centuries are thick, dark waves that rise and fall, steeped in blood. Every moment is a gaping abyss.*

✿   17. *Gaze on the dark sea without staggering, confront the abyss every moment without illusion or impudence or fear.*

WITHOUT ILLUSION, *impudence, or fear. But this is not enough; take a further step: battle to give meaning to the confused struggles of man.*

✿   19. *Train your heart to govern as spacious an arena as it can. Encompass through one century, then through two centuries, through three, through ten, through as many centuries as you can bear, the onward march of mankind. Train your eye to gaze on people moving in great stretches of time.*

✿   20. *Immerse yourself in this vision with patience, with love and high disinterestedness, until slowly the world begins to breathe within you, the embattled begin to be enlightened, to unite in your heart and to acknowledge themselves as brothers.*

✿   21. *The heart unites whatever the mind separates, pushes on beyond the arena of necessity and transmutes the struggle into love.*

✿   22. *Walk tiptoe on the edge of the insatiable precipice and struggle to give order to your vision. Raise the multicolored trap door of the* mystery—the stars, the sea, men and ideas; give form and meaning to the formless, the mindless infinitude.

☼ 23. Gather together in your heart all terrors, recompose all details. Salvation is a circle; close it!

☼ 24. What is meant by happiness? To live every unhappiness. What is meant by light? To gaze with undimmed eyes on all darknesses.

☼ 25. We are a humble letter, a single syllable, one word out of a gigantic Odyssey. We are immersed in an enormous song and we shine like humble pebbles as long as they remain immersed in the sea.

☼ 26. What is our duty? To raise our heads from the text a moment, as long as our lungs can bear it, and to breathe in the transoceanic song.

☼ 27. To bring together all our adventures, to give meaning to our voyage, to battle undauntedly with men, with gods, with animals, and then slowly, patiently, to erect in our brains, marrow of our marrow, our Ithaca.

☼ 28. Out of an ocean of nothingness, with fearful struggle, the work of man rises slowly like a small island.

☼ 29. Within this arena, which grows more stable night after day, generations work and love and hope and vanish. New generations tread on the corpses of their fathers, continue the work above the abyss and struggle to tame the dread mystery. How? By cultivating a single field, by

79

kissing a woman, by studying a stone, an animal, an idea.

※ 30. Earthquakes come, the island sways, a corner crumbles away, another rises out of the sunless waves.

※ 31. The mind is a seafaring laborer whose work is to build a seawall in chaos.

※ 32. From all these generations, from all these joys and sorrows, from this lovemaking, these battles, these ideas, a single voice rings out, pure and serene. Pure and serene because, though it contains all the sins and disquietudes of struggling man, it yet flies beyond them all and mounts higher still.

※ 33. Amidst all this human material Someone clambers up on his hands and knees, drowned in tears and blood, struggling to save himself.

※ 34. To save himself from whom? From the body which entwines him, from the people who support him, from the flesh, from the heart and the brains of man.

※ 35. "Lord, who are you? You loom before me like a Centaur, his hands stretched toward the sky, his feet transfixed in mud."

"I am He who eternally ascends."

"Why do you ascend? You strain every muscle, you struggle and fight to emerge from the beast. From the beast, and from man. Do not leave me!"

"I fight and ascend that I may not drown. I stretch out my hands, I clutch at every warm body, I raise my head above my brains that I may breathe. I drown everywhere and can nowhere be contained."

"Lord, why do you tremble?"

"I am afraid! This dark ascent has no ending. My head is a flame that tries eternally to detach itself, but the breath of night blows eternally to put me out. My struggle is endangered every moment. My struggle is endangered in every body. I walk and stumble in the flesh like a traveler overtaken by night, and I call out: 'Help me!' "

Fourth Step

THE EARTH

IT IS NOT you who call. It is not your voice calling from within your ephemeral breast. It is not only the white, yellow, and black generations of man calling in your heart. The entire Earth, with her trees and her waters, with her animals, with her men and her gods, calls from within your breast.

2. Earth rises up in your brains and sees her entire body for the first time.

✸ 3. *She shudders; she is a beast that eats, begets, moves, remembers. She hungers, she devours her children—plants, animals, men, thoughts—she grinds them in her dark jaws, passes them through her body once more, then casts them again into the soil.*

✸ 4. *She recalls her passions and broods upon them. Her memory unfolds within my heart, it spreads everywhere and conquers time.*

✸ 5. *It is not the heart which leaps and throbs in the blood. It is the entire Earth. She turns her gaze backward and relives her dread ascent through chaos.*

✸ 6. *I recall an endless desert of infinite and flaming matter. I am burning! I pass through immeasurable, unorganized time, completely alone, despairing, crying in the wilderness.*

✸ 7. *And slowly the flame subsides, the womb of matter grows cool, the stone comes alive, breaks open, and a small green leaf uncurls into the air, trembling. It clutches the soil, steadies itself, raises its head and hands, grasps the air, the water, the light, and sucks at the Universe.*

✸ 8. *It sucks at the Universe and wants to pass it through its body—thin as a thread—to turn it into flower, fruit, seed. To make it deathless.*

✸ 9. *The sea shudders and is torn in two; out of its muddy depths a voracious, restless, and eyeless worm ascends.*

✸ 10. *The weight of matter is conquered, the slab of death heaves high, and armies of trees and* beasts emerge filled with lust and hunger.

⚙ 11. *I gaze upon Earth with her muddy brain, and I shudder as I relive the peril. I might have sunk and vanished amid these roots that suck at the mud blissfully; I might have smothered in this tough and many-wrinkled hide; or I might have twitched eternally within the bloody, dark skull of the primordial ancestor.*

⚙ 12. *But I was saved. I passed beyond the thick-leaved plants, I passed beyond the fishes, the birds, the beasts, the apes. I created man.*

⚙ 13. *I created man, and now I struggle to be rid of him.*

⚙ 14. *"I am cramped and crushed! I want to escape!" This cry destroys and fructifies the bowels of the earth eternally. It leaps from body to body, from generation to generation, from species to species, becoming always stronger and more carnivorous. All parents shout: "I want to give birth to a son greater than I!"*

⚙ 15. *During those fearful moments when the Cry passes through our bodies, we feel a prehuman power driving us ruthlessly. Behind us a muddy torrent roars, full of blood, tears, and sweat, filled with squeals of joy, of lust, of death.*

⚙ 16. *An erotic wind blows over Earth, a giddiness overpowers all living creatures till they unite in the sea, in caves, in the air, under the ground, transferring from body to body a great, incomprehensible message.*

⚙ 17. *Only now, as we feel the onslaught be-*

hind us, do we begin dimly to apprehend why the animals fought, begot, and died; and behind them the plants; and behind these the huge reserve of inorganic forces.

⚙ 18. We are moved by pity, gratitude, and esteem for our old comrades-in-arms. They toiled, loved, and died to open a road for our coming.

⚙ 19. We also toil with the same delight, agony, and exaltation for the sake of Someone Else who with every courageous deed of ours proceeds one step farther.

⚙ 20. All our struggle once more will have a purpose much greater than we, wherein our toils, our miseries, and our crimes will have become useful and holy.

⚙ 21. This is an onslaught! A Spirit [30] rushes, storms through matter and fructifies it, passes beyond the animals, creates man, digs its claws into his head like a vulture, and shrieks.

⚙ 22. It is our turn now. It molds us, pummels matter within us and turns it into spirit, tramples on our brains, mounts astride our sperm, kicks our bodies behind it, and struggles to escape.

⚙ 23. It is as though the whole of life were the visible, eternal pursuit of an invisible Bridegroom who from body to body hunts down his untamed Bride, Eternity.

⚙ 24. And we, all the guests of the wedding procession—plants, animals, men—rush trembling toward the mystical nuptial chamber. We each carry with awe the sacred symbols of marriage— one the Phallos, another the Womb.

84

The Vision

YOU HEARD *the Cry and set forth. From battle to battle you passed through all the war service of militant man.*

❁ *2. You fought within the small tent of your body, but behold, the battle arena seemed too narrow; you felt stifled and rushed out to escape.*

❁ *3. You pitched your camp on your race, you brimmed with hands and hearts as with your blood you first revived the dread ancestors and then set forth with the dead, the living, and the unborn to give battle.*

❁ *4. Suddenly all races moved with you, the holy army of man was arranged for battle behind you, and all earth resounded like a military encampment.*

87

✸ 5. You climbed to a high peak from which the plan of battle branched out amid the coils of your brain, and all opposing expeditions united in the secret encampment of your heart.

✸ 6. Behind you the plants and animals were organized like supply troops for the front-line battling armies of man.

✸ 7. Now entire Earth clings to you, becomes flesh of your flesh, and cries out of chaos.

ＨOW CAN I besiege this dread vision with words? I stoop over chaos and listen. Someone is groaning and climbing up a secret, dangerous slope.

✸ 9. He struggles and agonizes stubbornly to ascend. But he finds a contrary force that impedes him: Someone is hurriedly climbing down a secret and easy downward slope.

✸ 10. Within the descending sluggish stream the Spirit is dismembered and whirled about, and for a moment—the duration of every life—the two opposing desires are balanced.

✸ 11. This is how bodies are born, how the world is created, how among living things the two antithetical powers find equilibrium.

✸ 12. For a moment the One ascending is entwined by a beloved body—his own body—and is retarded in his climbing. But quickly, with love, *with death, he escapes it, and then continues to plod on.*

☼ 13. *He tramples on inorganic matter, he shapes the plant and fills it. He encamps in it with his whole being. By "his whole being" is meant together with the longing and the power to escape.*

☼ 14. *He emerges a little, breathes with difficulty, chokes. He abandons to the plants as much heaviness, as much stupor and immobility as he can and, thus disburdened, leaps, with his whole being again, farther and higher still, creating the animals and encamping in their loins.*

☼ 15. *Again, "with his whole being" means together with the longing and the power to escape.*

☼ 16. *The bodies breathe, feed, store up strength, and then in an erotic moment are shattered, are spent and drained utterly, that they may bequeath their spirit to their sons. What spirit? The drive upward!*

☼ 17. *He purifies himself slowly by struggling amid their bodies, and abandons to the animals as much passion, as much slavishness, as much impotence and darkness as he can.*

☼ 18. *Then once more he rises slightly, a bit lighter, and rushes to escape. It is this drive toward freedom, this strife with matter, which slowly creates the head of man.*

☼ 19. *And now we feel with terror that he is again struggling to escape beyond us, to cast us* off with plants and animals, and to leap farther. The moment has come—O great joy and bitterness!—when we, the vanquished, must also be cast away among the reserve troops.

✲ 20. Behind the stream of my mind and body, behind the stream of my race and all mankind, behind the stream of plants and animals, I watch with trembling the Invisible, treading on all visible things and ascending.

✲ 21. Behind his heavy and blood-splattered feet I hear all living things being trampled on and crushed.

✲ 22. His face is without laughter, dark and silent, beyond joy and sorrow, beyond hope.

✲ 23. I tremble. Are YOU my God? Your body is steeped in memory. Like one locked up in dungeons for many years, you have adorned your arms and chest with strange trees and hairy dragons, with gory adventures, with cries and chronologies.

✲ 24. Lord, my Lord, you growl like a wild beast! Your feet are covered with blood and mire, your hands are covered with blood and mire, your jaws are heavy millstones that grind slowly.

✲ 25. You clutch at trees and animals, you tread on man, you shout. You climb up the endless black precipice of death, and you tremble.

✲ 26. Where are you going? Pain increases, the light and the darkness increase. You weep, you hook onto me, you feed on my blood, you grow huge and strong, and then you kick at my heart. I press you to my breast, and I fear you and pity you.

✿ 27. It is as though we had buried Someone we thought dead, and now hear him calling in the night: Help me! Heaving and panting, he raises the gravestone of our soul and body higher and still higher, breathing more freely at every moment.

✿ 28. Every word, every deed, every thought is the heavy gravestone he is forever trying to lift. And my own body and all the visible world, all heaven and earth, are the gravestone which God is struggling to heave upward.

✿ 29. Trees shout, animals and stars: "We are doomed!" Every living creature flings two huge hands as high as the heavens to seek help.

✿ 30. With his knees doubled up under his chin, with his hands spread toward the light, with the soles of his feet turned toward his back, God huddles in a knot in every cell of flesh.

✿ 31. When I break a fruit open, this is how every seed is revealed to me. When I speak to men, this what I discern in their thick and muddy brains.

✿ 32. God struggles in every thing, his hands flung upward toward the light. What light? Beyond and above every thing!

P AIN IS NOT *the only essence of our God, nor is hope in a future life or a life on this earth, neither joy nor victory. Every religion that holds up to worship one of these primordial aspects of God narrows our hearts and our minds.*

✿ 34. *The essence of our God is* STRUGGLE. *Pain, joy, and hope unfold and labor within this struggle, world without end.*

✿ 35. *It is this ascension, the battle with the descending countercurrent, which gives birth to pain. But pain is not the absolute monarch. Every victory, every momentary balance on the ascent fills with joy every living thing that breathes, grows, loves, and gives birth.*

✿ 36. *But from every joy and pain a hope leaps out eternally to escape this pain and to widen joy.*

✿ 37. *And again the ascent begins—which is pain—and joy is reborn and new hope springs up once more. The circle never closes. It is not a circle, but a spiral which ascends eternally, ever widening, enfolding and unfolding the triune struggle.*

W HAT IS THE *purpose of this struggle? This is what the wretched self-seeking mind of man is always asking, forgetting that the Great Spirit* does not toil within the bounds of human time, place, or casualty.

☼ 39. The Great Spirit is superior to these human questionings. It teems with many rich and wandering drives which to our shallow minds seem contradictory; but in the essence of divinity they fraternize and struggle together, faithful comrades-in-arms.

☼ 40. The primordial Spirit branches out, overflows, struggles, fails, succeeds, trains itself. It is the Rose of the Winds.[31]

☼ 41. Whether we want to or not, we also sail on and voyage, consciously or unconsciously, amid divine endeavors. Indeed, even our march has eternal elements, without beginning or end, assisting God and sharing His perils.

☼ 42. Which is that one force amid all of God's forces which man is able to grasp? Only this: We discern a crimson line on this earth, a red, blood-splattered line which ascends, struggling, from matter to plants, from plants to animals, from animals to man.

☼ 43. This indestructible prehuman rhythm is the only visible journey of the Invisible on this earth. Plants, animals, and men are the steps which God creates on which to tread and to mount upward.

☼ 44. Difficult, dreadful, unending ascension! Shall God conquer or be conquered in this onslaught? Does victory exist? Does defeat exist?

Our bodies shall rot and turn to dust, but what will become of Him who for a moment passed beyond the body?

⚙ 45. Yet these are all lesser concerns, for all hopes and despairs vanish in the voracious, funneling whirlwind of God. God laughs, wails, kills, sets us on fire, and then leaves us in the middle of the way, charred embers.

⚙ 46. And I rejoice to feel between my temples, in the flicker of an eyelid, the beginning and the end of the world.

⚙ 47. I condense into a lightning moment the seeding, sprouting, blossoming, fructifying, and the disappearance of every tree, animal, man, star, and god.

⚙ 48. All Earth is a seed planted in the coils of my mind. Whatever struggles for numberless years to unfold and fructify in the dark womb of matter bursts in my head like a small and silent lightning flash.

⚙ 49. Ah! let us gaze intently on this lightning flash, let us hold it for a moment, let us arrange it into human speech.

⚙ 50. Let us transfix this momentary eternity which encloses everything, past and future, but without losing in the immobility of language any of its gigantic erotic whirling.

⚙ 51. Every word is an Ark of the Covenant around which we dance and shudder, divining God to be its dreadful inhabitant.

⚙ 52. You shall never be able to establish in

words that you live in ecstasy. But struggle unceasingly to establish it in words. Battle with myths, with comparisons, with allegories, with rare and common words, with exclamations and rhymes, to embody it in flesh, to transfix it!

⚙ *53. God, the Great Ecstatic, works in the same way. He speaks and struggles to speak in every way He can, with seas and with fires, with colors, with wings, with horns, with claws, with constellations and butterflies, that he may establish His ecstasy.*

⚙ *54. Like every other living thing, I also am in the center of the Cosmic whirlpool. I am the eye of monstrous rivers where everything dances about me as the circle continually narrows with greater vehemence till the heavens and earth plunge into the red pit of my heart.*

⚙ *55. Then God confronts me with terror and love—for I am His only hope—and says: "This Ecstatic, who gives birth to all things, who rejoices in them all and yet destroys them, this Ecstatic is my Son!"*

The Action

The Relationship Between God and Man

THE ULTIMATE *most holy form of theory is action.*

※ *2. Not to look on passively while the spark leaps from generation to generation, but to leap and to burn with it!*

※ *3. Action is the widest gate of deliverance. It alone can answer the questionings of the heart. Amid the labyrinthine complexities of the mind it finds the shortest route. No, it does not "find" —it creates its way, hewing to right and left through resistances of logic and matter.*

※ *4. Why did you struggle behind phenomena to track down the Invisible? What was the purpose of all your warlike, your erotic march through flesh, race, man, plants, and animals?*

99

Why the mystic marriage beyond these labors, the perfect embracement, the bacchic and raging contact in darkness and in light?

☼ *5. That you might reach the point from which you began—the ephemeral, palpitating, mysterious point of your existence—with new eyes, with new ears, with a new sense of taste, smell, touch, with new brains.*

☼ *6. Our profound human duty is not to interpret or to cast light on the rhythm of God's march, but to adjust, as much as we can, the rhythm of our small and fleeting life to his.*

☼ *7. Only thus may we mortals succeed in achieving something immortal, because then we collaborate with One who is Deathless.*

☼ *8. Only thus may we conquer mortal sin, the concentration on details, the narrowness of our brains; only thus may we transubstantiate into freedom the slavery of earthen matter given us to mold.*

☼ *9. Amid all these things, beyond all these things every man and nation, every plant and animal, every god and demon, charges upward like an army inflamed by an incomprehensible, unconquerable Spirit.*

☼ *10. We struggle to make this Spirit visible, to give it a face, to encase it in words, in allegories and thoughts and incantations, that it may not escape us.*

☼ *11. But it cannot be contained in the twenty-six letters of an alphabet which we string out in* rows; we know that all these words, these allegories, these thoughts, and these incantations are, once more, but a new mask with which to conceal the Abyss.

☼   12. Yet only in this manner, by confining immensity, may we labor within the newly incised circle of humanity.

☼   13. What do we mean by "labor"? To fill up this circle with desires, with anxieties, and with deeds; to spread out and reach frontiers until, no longer able to contain us, they crack and collapse. By thus working with appearances, we widen and increase the essence.

☼   14. For this reason our return to appearances, after our contact with essence, possesses an incalculable worth.

☼   15. We have seen the highest circle of spiraling powers. We have named this circle God. We might have given it any other name we wished: Abyss, Mystery, Absolute Darkness, Absolute Light, Matter, Spirit, Ultimate Hope, Ultimate Despair, Silence.

☼   16. But we have named it God because only this name, for primordial reasons, can stir our hearts profoundly. And this deeply felt emotion is indispensable if we are to touch, body with body, the dread essence beyond logic.

☼   17. Within this gigantic circle of divinity we are in duty bound to separate and perceive clearly the small, burning arc of our epoch.

☼   18. On this barely perceptible flaming curve,

feeling the onrush of the entire circle profoundly and mystically, we travel in harmony with the Universe, we gain impetus and dash into battle.

✷ 19. *Thus, by consciously following the on-rush of the Universe, our ephemeral action does not die with us.*

✷ 20. *It does not become lost in a mystical and passive contemplation of the entire circle; it does not scorn holy, humble, and daily necessity.*

✷ 21. *Within its narrow and blood-drenched ditch it stoops and labors steadfastly, conquering easily both space and time within a small point of space and time—for this point follows the divine onrush of the entire circle.*

✷ 22. *I do not care what face other ages and other people have given to the enormous, faceless essence. They have crammed it with human vir-tues, with rewards and punishments, with certain-ties. They have given a face to their hopes and fears, they have submitted their anarchy to a rhythm, they have found a higher justification by which to live and labor. They have fulfilled their duty.*

✷ 23. *But today we have gone beyond these needs; we have shattered this particular mask of the Abyss; our God no longer fits under the old features.*

✷ 24. *Our hearts have overbrimmed with new agonies, with new luster and silence. The mystery has grown savage, and God has grown greater. The dark powers ascend, for they have also grown greater, and the entire human island quakes.*

☼ 25. *Let us stoop down to our hearts and confront the Abyss valiantly. Let us try to mold once more, with our flesh and blood, the new, contemporary face of God.*

☼ 26. *For our God is not an abstract thought, a logical necessity, a high and harmonious structure made of deductions and speculations.*

☼ 27. *He is not an immaculate, neutral, odorless, distilled product of our brains, neither male nor female.*

☼ 28. *He is both man and woman, mortal and immortal, dung and spirit. He gives birth, fecundates, slaughters—death and eros in one—and then he begets and slays once more, dancing spaciously beyond the boundaries of a logic which cannot contain the antinomies.*

☼ 29. *My God is not Almighty. He struggles, for he is in peril every moment; he trembles and stumbles in every living thing, and he cries out. He is defeated incessantly, but rises again, full of blood and earth, to throw himself into battle once more.*

☼ 30. *He is full of wounds, his eyes are filled with fear and stubbornness, his jawbones and temples are splintered. But he does not surrender, he ascends; he ascends with his feet, with his hands, biting his lips, undaunted.*

☼ 31. *My God is not All-holy. He is full of cruelty and savage justice, and he chooses the best mercilessly. He is without compassion; he does* not trouble himself about men or animals; nor does he care for virtues and ideas. He loves all these things for a moment, then smashes them eternally and passes on.

✿ 32. He is a power that contains all things, that begets all things. He begets them, loves them, and destroys them. And if we say, "Our God is an erotic wind and shatters all bodies that he may drive on," and if we remember that eros always works through blood and tears, destroying every individual without mercy—then we shall approach his dread face a little closer.

✿ 33. My God is not All-knowing. His brain is a tangled skein of light and darkness which he strives to unravel in the labyrinth of the flesh.

✿ 34. He stumbles and fumbles. He gropes to the right and turns back; swings to the left and sniffs the air. He struggles above chaos in anguish. Crawling, straining, groping for unnumbered centuries, he feels the muddy coils of his brain being slowly suffused with light.

✿ 35. On the surface of his heavy, pitch-black head he begins with an indescribable struggle to create eyes by which to see, ears by which to hear.

✿ 36. My God struggles on without certainty. Will he conquer? Will he be conquered? Nothing in the Universe is certain. He flings himself into uncertainty; he gambles all his destiny at every moment.

✿ 37. He clings to warm bodies; he has no other bulwark. He shouts for help; he proclaims *a mobilization throughout the Universe.*

☼   38. *It is our duty, on hearing his Cry, to run under his flag, to fight by his side, to be lost or to be saved with him.*

☼   39. *God is imperiled. He is not almighty, that we may cross our hands, waiting for certain victory. He is not all-holy, that we may wait trustingly for him to pity and to save us.*

☼   40. *Within the province of our ephemeral flesh all of God is imperiled. He cannot be saved unless we save him with our own struggles; nor can we be saved unless he is saved.*

☼   41. *We are one. From the blind worm in the depths of the ocean to the endless arena of the Galaxy, only one person struggles and is imperiled: You. And within your small and earthen breast only one thing struggles and is imperiled: the Universe.*

W<small>E MUST UNDERSTAND</small> *well that we do not proceed from a unity of God to the same unity of God again. We do not proceed from one chaos to another chaos, neither from one light to another light, nor from one darkness to another darkness. What would be the value of our life then? What would be the value of all life?*

☼   43. *But we set out from an almighty chaos, from a thick abyss of light and darkness tangled. And we struggle—plants, animals, men, ideas— in this momentary passage of individual life, to* put in order the Chaos within us, to cleanse the abyss, to work upon as much darkness as we can within our bodies and to transmute it into light.

⚙ 44. We do not struggle for ourselves, nor for our race, not even for humanity.

⚙ 45. We do not struggle for Earth, nor for ideas. All these are the precious yet provisional stairs of our ascending God, and they crumble away as soon as he steps upon them in his ascent.

⚙ 46. In the smallest lightning flash of our lives, we feel all of God treading upon us, and suddenly we understand: if we all desire it intensely, if we organize all the visible and invisible powers of earth and fling them upward, if we all battle together like fellow combatants eternally vigilant—then the Universe might possibly be saved.

⚙ 47. It is not God who will save us—it is we who will save God, by battling, by creating, and by transmuting matter into spirit.

⚙ 48. But all our struggle may go lost. If we tire, if we grow faint of spirit, if we fall into panic, then the entire Universe becomes imperiled.

⚙ 49. Life is a crusade in the service of God. Whether we wished to or not, we set out as crusaders to free—not the Holy Sepulchre—but that God buried in matter and in our souls.

⚙ 50. Every body, every soul is a Holy Sepulchre. Every seed of grain is a Holy Sepulchre; let *us free it! The brain is a Holy Sepulchre, God sprawls within it and battles with death; let us run to his assistance!*

☼ 51. *God gives the signal for battle, and I, too, rush to the attack, trembling.*

☼ 52. *Whether I straggle behind as a deserter or battle valiantly, I know that I shall always fall in battle. But on the first occasion my death would be sterile, for with the destruction of my body my soul would also be lost and scattered to the winds.*

☼ 53. *On the second occasion, I would descend into earth like a fruit brimming with seed. Though my breath abandon my body to rot, it would organize new bodies and continue the battle.*

☼ 54. *My prayer is not the whimpering of a beggar nor a confession of love. Nor is it the trivial reckoning of a small tradesman: Give me and I shall give you.*

☼ 55. *My prayer is the report of a soldier to his general: This is what I did today, this is how I fought to save the entire battle in my own sector, these are the obstacles I found, this is how I plan to fight tomorrow.*

☼ 56. *My God and I are horsemen galloping in the burning sun or under drizzling rain. Pale, starving, but unsubdued, we ride and converse.*

☼ 57. *"Leader!" I cry. He turns his face toward me, and I shudder to confront his anguish.*

☼ 58. *Our love for each other is rough and ready, we sit at the same table, we drink the same wine in this low tavern of life.*

☼ 59. *As we clink our glasses, swords clash and resound, loves and hates spring up. We get drunk, visions of slaughter ascend before our eyes, cities crumble and fall in our brains, and though we are both wounded and screaming with pain, we plunder a huge Palace.*

The Relationship Between Man and Man

WHAT IS *the essence of our God? The struggle for freedom. In the indestructible darkness a flaming line ascends and emblazons the march of the Invisible. What is our duty? To ascend with this blood-drenched line.*

☼ 2. *Whatever rushes upward and helps God to ascend is good. Whatever drags downward and impedes God from ascending is evil.*

☼ 3. *All virtues and all evils take on a new*

value. They are freed from the moment and from earth, they exist completely within man, before and after man, eternally.

⚙ *4. For the essence of our ethic is not the salvation of man, who varies within time and space, but the salvation of God, who within a wide variety of flowing human forms and adventures is always the same, the indestructible rhythm which battles for freedom.*

⚙ *5. We, as human beings, are all miserable persons, heartless, small, insignificant. But within us a superior essence drives us ruthlessly upward.*

⚙ *6. From within this human mire divine songs have welled up, great ideas, violent loves, an unsleeping assault full of mystery, without beginning or end, without purpose, beyond every purpose.*

⚙ *7. Humanity is such a lump of mud, each one of us is such a lump of mud. What is our duty? To struggle so that a small flower may blossom from the dunghill of our flesh and mind.*

⚙ *8. Out of things and flesh, out of hunger, out of fear, out of virtue and sin, struggle continually to create God.*

⚙ *9. How does the light of a star set out and plunge into black eternity in its immortal course? The star dies, but the light never dies; such also is the cry of freedom.*

⚙ *10. Out of the transient encounter of contrary forces which constitute your existence, strive* to create whatever immortal thing a mortal may create in this world—a Cry.

⚙ 11. And this Cry, abandoning to the earth the body which gave it birth, proceeds and labors eternally.

A VEHEMENT EROS *runs through the Universe. It is like the ether: harder than steel, softer than air.*

⚙ 13. *It cuts through and passes beyond all things, it flees and escapes. It does not repose in warm detail nor enslave itself in the beloved body. It is a Militant Eros. Behind the shoulders of its beloved it perceives mankind surging and roaring like waves, it perceives animals and plants uniting and dying, it perceives the Lord imperiled and shouting to it: "Save me!"*

⚙ 14. *Eros? What other name may we give that impetus which becomes enchanted as soon as it casts its glance on matter and then longs to impress its features upon it? It confronts the body and longs to pass beyond it, to merge with the other erotic cry hidden in that body, to become one till both may vanish and become deathless by begetting sons.*

⚙ 15. *It approaches the soul and wishes to merge with it inseparably so that "you" and "I" may no longer exist; it blows on the mass of man-*

kind and wishes, by smashing the resistances of mind and body, to merge all breaths into one violent gale that may lift the earth!

⚙ 16. In moments of crisis this Erotic Love swoops down on men and joins them together by force—friends and foes, good and evil. It is a breath superior to all of them, independent of their desires and deeds. It is the spirit, the breathing of God on earth.

⚙ 17. It descends on men in whatever form it wishes—as dance, as eros, as hunger, as religion, as slaughter. It does not ask our permission.

⚙ 18. In these hours of crisis God struggles to knead flesh and brains together in the trough of earth, to cast all this mass of dough into the merciless whirlwind of his rotation and to give it a face—his face.

⚙ 19. He does not choke with disgust, he does not despair in the dark, earthen entrails of men. He toils, proceeds, and devours the flesh; he clings to the belly, the heart, the mind and the phallos of man.

⚙ 20. He is not the upright head of a family; he does not portion out either bread or brains equally to his children. Injustice, Cruelty, Longing, and Hunger are the four steeds that drive his chariot on this rough-hewn earth of ours.

⚙ 21. God is never created out of happiness or comfort or glory, but out of shame and hunger and tears.

AT EVERY MOMENT of crisis an array of men risk their lives in the front ranks as standard-bearers of God to fight and take upon themselves the whole responsibility of the battle.

23. Once long ago it was the priests, the kings, the noblemen, or the burghers who created civilizations and set divinity free.

24. Today God is the common worker made savage by toil and rage and hunger. He stinks of smoke and wine and meat. He swears and hungers and begets children; he cannot sleep; he shouts and threatens in the cellars and garrets of earth.

25. The air has changed, and we breathe in deeply a spring laden and filled with seed. Cries rise up on every side. Who shouts? It is we who shout—the living, the dead, and the unborn. But at once we are crushed by fear, and we fall silent.

26. And then we forget—out of laziness, out of habit, out of cowardice. But suddenly the Cry tears at our entrails once more, like an eagle.

27. For the Cry is not outside us, it does not come from a great distance that we may escape it. It sits in the center of our hearts, and cries out.

28. God shouts: "Burn your houses! I am coming! Whoever has a house cannot receive me!

☼ 29. "Burn your ideas, smash your thoughts! Whoever has found the solution cannot find me.

☼ 30. "I love the hungry, the restless, the vagabonds. They are the ones who brood eternally on hunger, on rebellion, on the endless road—on ME!

☼ 31. "I am coming! Leave your wives, your children, your ideas, and follow me. I am the great Vagabond.

☼ 32. "Follow! Stride over joy and sorrow, over peace and justice and virtue! Forward! Smash these idols, smash them all, they cannot contain me. Smash even yourself that I may pass."

☼ 33. Set fire! This is our great duty today amid such immoral and hopeless chaos.

☼ 34. War against the unbelievers! The unbelievers are the satisfied, the satiated, the sterile.

☼ 35. Our hate is uncompromising because it knows that it works for love better and more profoundly than any weak-hearted kindness.

☼ 36. We hate, we are never content, we are unjust, we are cruel and filled with restlessness and faith; we seek the impossible, like lovers.

☼ 37. Sow fire to purify the earth! Let a more dreadful abyss open up between good and evil, let injustice increase, let Hunger descend to thresh our bowels, for we may not otherwise be saved.

☼ 38. We are living in a critical, violent moment of history; an entire world is crashing down,

113

another has not yet been born. Our epoch is not a moment of equilibrium in which refinement, reconciliation, peace, and love might be fruitful virtues.

✤ *39. We live in a moment of dread assault, we stride over our enemies, we stride over our lagging friends, we are imperiled in the midst of chaos, we drown. We can no longer fit into old virtues and hopes, into old theories and actions.*

✤ *40. The wind of devastation is blowing; this is the breath of our God today; let us be carried away in its tide! The wind of devastation is the first dancing surge of the creative rotation. It blows over every head and every city, it knocks down houses and ideas, it passes over desolate wastes, and it shouts: "Prepare yourselves! War! It's War!"*

✤ *41. This is our epoch, good or bad, beautiful or ugly, rich or poor—we did not choose it. This is our epoch, the air we breathe, the mud given us, the bread, the fire, the spirit!*

✤ *42. Let us accept Necessity courageously. It is our lot to have fallen on fighting times. Let us tighten our belts, let us arm our hearts, our minds, and our bodies. Let us take our place in battle!*

✤ *43. War is the lawful sovereign of our age. Today the only complete and virtuous man is the warrior. For only he, faithful to the great pulse of our time, smashing, hating, desiring, follows the present command of our God.*

THIS IDENTIFICATION of ourselves with the Universe begets the two superior virtues of our ethics: responsibility and sacrifice.

☼ 45. It is our duty to help liberate that God who is stifling in us, in mankind, in masses of people living in darkness.

☼ 46. We must be ready at any moment to give up our lives for his sake. For life is not a goal; it is also an instrument, like death, like beauty, like virtue, like knowledge. Whose instrument? Of that God who fights for freedom.

☼ 47. We are all one, we are all an imperiled essence. If at the far end of the world a spirit degenerates, it drags down our spirit into its own degradation. If one mind at the far end of the world sinks into idiocy, our own temples overbrim with darkness.

☼ 48. For it is only One who struggles at the far end of earth and sky. One. And if He goes lost, it is we who must bear the responsibility. If He goes lost, then we go lost.

☼ 49. This is why the salvation of the Universe is also our salvation, why solidarity among men is no longer a tenderhearted luxury but a deep necessity and self-preservation, as much a necessity as, in an army under fire, the salvation of your comrade-in-arms.

☀ 50. But our morality ascends even higher. We are all one army under fire. Yet we have no certain knowledge that we shall conquer, we have no certain knowledge that we shall be conquered.

☀ 51. Does salvation exist, does a purpose exist which we serve and in the service of which we shall find deliverance?

☀ 52. Or is there no salvation, is there no purpose, are all things in vain and our contribution of no value at all?

☀ 53. Neither one nor the other. Our God is not almighty, he is not all-holy, he is not certain that he will conquer, he is not certain that he will be conquered.

☀ 54. The essence of our God is obscure. It ripens continuously; perhaps victory is strenghened with our every valorous deed, but perhaps even all these agonizing struggles toward deliverance and victory are inferior to the nature of divinity.

☀ 55. Whatever it might be, we fight on without certainty, and our virtue, uncertain of any rewards, acquires a profound nobility.

☀ 56. All the commandments are put to rout. We do not see, we do not hear, we do not hate, we do not love as once we did. Earth takes on a new virginity. Bread and water and women take on a new flavor. Action takes on a new, incalculable value.

☀ 57. All acquire an unexpected holiness—beauty, knowledge, hope, the economic struggle,

daily and seemingly meaningless cares. Shudder-
ing, we feel everywhere about us the same gigan-
tic, enslaved Spirit striving for freedom.

EVERYONE HAS *his own particular road which*
leads him to liberation—one the road of virtue,
another the road of evil.

⚙ 59. *If the road leading you to your liberation*
is that of disease, of lies, of dishonor, it is then
your duty to plunge into disease, into lies, into
dishonor, that you may conquer them. You may
not otherwise be saved.

⚙ 60. *If the road which leads you to your lib-*
eration is the road of virtue, of joy, of truth, it is
then your duty to plunge into virtue, into joy, into
truth, that you may conquer them and leave them
behind you. You may not otherwise be saved.

⚙ 61. *We do not fight our dark passions with*
a sober, bloodless, neutral virtue which rises
above passion, but with other, more violent pas-
sions.

⚙ 62. *We leave our door open to sin. We do*
not plug up our ears with wax that we may not
listen to the Sirens. We do not bind ourselves,
out of fear, to the mast of a great idea; nor by
hearing and by embracing the Sirens do we aban-
don our ship, and perish.

⚙ 63. *On the contrary, we seize the Sirens and*
pitch them into our boat so that even they may

voyage with us; and we continue on our way. This, my comrades, is our new Asceticism, our Spiritual Exercises!

❀ 64. God cries to my heart: "Save me!"

❀ 65. God cries to men, to animals, to plants, to matter: "Save me!"

❀ 66. Listen to your heart and follow him. Shatter your body and awake: We are all one.

❀ 67. Love man because you are he.

❀ 68. Love animals and plants because you were they, and now they follow you like faithful co-workers and slaves.

❀ 69. Love your body; only with it may you fight on this earth and turn matter into spirit.

❀ 70. Love matter. God clings to it tooth and nail, and fights. Fight with him.

❀ 71. Die every day. Be born every day. Deny everything you have every day. The superior virtue is not to be free but to fight for freedom.

❀ 72. Do not condescend to ask: "Shall we conquer? Shall we be conquered?" Fight on!

❀ 73. So may the enterprise of the Universe, for an ephemeral moment, for as long as you are alive, become your own enterprise. This, Comrades, is our new Decalogue.

The Relationship
Between
Man and Nature

ALL THIS WORLD, *all this rich, endless flow of appearances is not a deception, a multicolored phantasmagoria of our mirroring mind. Nor is it absolute reality which lives and evolves freely, independent of our mind's power.*

2. *It is not the resplendent robe which arrays the mystic body of God. Nor the obscurely translucent partition between man and mystery.*

3. *All this world that we see, hear, and touch is that accessible to the human senses, a condensation of the two enormous powers of the Universe permeated with all of God.*

4. *One power descends and wants to scatter, to come to a standstill, to die. The other power ascends and strives for freedom, for immortality.*

5. *These two armies, the dark and the light, the armies of life and of death, collide eternally. The visible signs of this collision are, for us, plants, animals, men.*

⚙ 6. *The antithetical powers collide eternally; they meet, fight, conquer and are conquered, become reconciled for a brief moment, and then begin to battle again throughout the Universe— from the invisible whirlpool in a drop of water to the endless cataclysm of stars in the Galaxy.*

⚙ 7. *Even the most humble insect and the most insignificant idea are the military encampments of God. Within them, all of God is arranged in fighting position for a critical battle.*

⚙ 8. *Even in the most meaningless particle of earth and sky I hear God crying out: "Help me!"*

⚙ 9. *Everything is an egg in which God's sperm labors without rest, ceaselessly. Innumerable forces within and without it range themselves to defend it.*

⚙ 10. *With the light of the brain, with the flame of the heart, I besiege every cell where God is jailed, seeking, trying, hammering to open a gate in the fortress of matter, to create a gap through which God may issue in heroic attack.*

Lie in ambush *behind appearances, patiently, and strive to subject them to laws. Thus may you open up roads through chaos and help the spirit on its course.*

⚙ 12. *Impose order, the order of your brain, on the flowing anarchy of the world. Incise your plan of battle clearly on the face of the abyss.*

☼ 13. *Contend with the powers of nature, force them to the yoke of superior purpose. Free that spirit which struggles within them and longs to mingle with that spirit which struggles within you.*

☼ 14. *When a man fighting with chaos subdues a series of appearances to the laws of his mind and strictly confines these laws within the boundaries of reason, then the world breathes, the voices are ranged in order, the future becomes clarified, and all the dark and endless quantities of numbers are freed by submitting to mystical quality.*

☼ 15. *With the help of our minds we compel matter to come with us. We divert the direction of descending powers, we alter the course of the current, we transform slavery into freedom.*

☼ 16. *We do not only free God by battling and subduing the visible world about us; we also create God.*

☼ 17. *"Open your eyes," God shouts; "I want to see! Prick up your ears, I want to hear! March in the front ranks: you are my head!"*

☼ 18. *A stone is saved if we lift it from the mire and build it into a house, or if we chisel the spirit upon it.*

☼ 19. *The seed is saved—what do we mean by "saved"? It frees the God within it by blossoming, by bearing fruit, by returning to earth once more. Let us help the seed to save itself.*

☼ 20. *Every man has his own circle composed*

of trees, animals, men, ideas, and he is in duty bound to save this circle. He, and no one else. If he does not save it, he cannot be saved.

✵ 21. These are the labors each man is given and is in duty bound to complete before he dies. He may not otherwise be saved. For his own soul is scattered and enslaved in these things about him, in trees, in animals, in men, in ideas, and it is his own soul he saves by completing these labors.

✵ 22. If you are a laborer, then till the earth, help it to bear fruit. The seeds in the earth cry out, and God cries out within the seeds. Set him free! A field awaits its deliverance at your hands, a machine awaits its soul. You may never be saved unless you save them.

✵ 23. If you are a warrior, be pitiless; compassion is not in the periphery of your duty. Kill the foe mercilessly. Hear how God cries out in the body of the enemy: "Kill this body, it obstructs me! Kill it that I may pass!"

✵ 24. If you are a man of learning, fight in the skull, kill ideas and create new ones. God hides in every idea as in every cell of flesh. Smash the idea, set him free! Give him another, a more spacious idea in which to dwell.

✵ 25. If you are a woman, then love. Choose austerely among all men the father of your children. It is not you who make the choice, but the indestructible, merciless, infinite, masculine God

within you. Fulfill all your duty, so overbrimming
with bitterness, love, and valor. Give up all your
body, so filled with blood and milk.

❀ 26. *Say: "This child, which I hold suckling*
at my breast, shall save God. Let me give him all
my blood and milk."

PROFOUND AND *incommensurable is the worth*
of this flowing world: God clings to it and ascends,
God feeds upon it and increases.

❀ 28. *My heart breaks open, my mind is*
flooded with light, and all at once this world's
dread battlefield is revealed to me as an erotic
arena.

❀ 29. *Two violent contrary winds, one mascu-*
line and the other feminine, met and clashed at
a crossroads. For a moment they counterbalanced
each other, thickened, and became visible.

❀ 30. *This crossroads is the Universe. This*
crossroads is my heart.

❀ 31. *This dance of the gigantic erotic colli-*
sion is transmitted from the darkest particle of
matter to the most spacious thought.

❀ 32. *The wife of my God is matter; they*
wrestle with each other, they laugh and weep,
they cry out in the nuptial bed of flesh.

❀ 33. *They spawn and are dismembered. They*
fill sea, land, and air with species of plants, ani-

mals, men, and spirits. This primordial pair embraces, is dismembered, and multiplies in every living creature.

✽ 34. All the concentrated agony of the Universe bursts out in every living thing. God is imperiled in the sweet ecstasy and bitterness of flesh.

✽ 35. But he shakes himself free, he leaps out of brains and loins, then clings to new brains and new loins until the struggle for liberation again breaks out from the beginning.

✽ 36. For the first time on this earth, from within our hearts and our minds, God gazes on his own struggle.

✽ 37. Joy! Joy! I did not know that all this world is so much part of me, that we are all one army, that windflowers and stars struggle to right and left of me and do not know me; but I turn to them and hail them.

✽ 38. The Universe is warm, beloved, familiar, and it smells like my own body. It is Love and War both, a raging restlessness, persistence and uncertainty.

✽ 39. Uncertainty and terror. In a violent flash of lightning I discern on the highest peak of power the final, the most fearful pair embracing: Terror and Silence. And between them, a Flame.

The Silence

THE SOUL OF MAN *is a flame, a bird of fire that leaps from bough to bough, from head to head, and that shouts: "I cannot stand still, I cannot be consumed, no one can quench me!"*

2. *All at once the Universe becomes a tree of fire. Amidst the smoke and the flames, reposing on the peak of conflagration, immaculate, cool, and serene, I hold that final fruit of fire, the Light.*

3. *From this lofty summit I look on the crimson line which ascends—a tremulous, bloodstained phosphorescence that drags itself like a lovesick insect through the raincool coils of my brain.*

4. *The ego, race, mankind, earth, theory*

and action, God—all these are phantasms made of loam and brain, good only for those simple hearts that live in fear, good only for those flatulent souls that imagine they are pregnant.

☼ 5. Where do we come from? Where are we going? What is the meaning of this life? That is what every heart is shouting, what every head is asking as it beats on chaos.

☼ 6. And a fire within me leaps up to answer: "Fire will surely come one day to purify the earth. Fire will surely come one day to obliterate the earth. This is the Second Coming.

☼ 7. "The soul is a flaming tongue that licks and struggles to set the black bulk of the world on fire. One day the entire Universe will become a single conflagration.

☼ 8. "Fire is the first and final mask of my God. We dance and weep between two enormous pyres."

☼ 9. Our thoughts and our bodies flash and glitter with reflected light. Between the two pyres I stand serenely, my brain unshaken amid the vertigo, and I say:

☼ 10. "Time is most short and space most narrow between these two pyres, the rhythm of this life is most sluggish, and I have no time, nor a place to dance in. I cannot wait."

☼ 11. Then all at once the rhythm of the earth becomes a vertigo, time disappears, the moment whirls, becomes eternity, and every point in space —insect or star or idea—turns into dance.

128

✺ 12. *It was a jail, and the jail was smashed, the dreadful powers within it were freed, and that point of space no longer exists!*

✺ 13. *This ultimate stage of our spiritual exercise is called Silence. Not because its contents are the ultimate inexpressible despair or the ultimate inexpressible joy and hope. Nor because it is the ultimate knowledge which does not condescend to speak, or the ultimate ignorance which cannot.*

✺ 14. *Silence means: Every person, after completing his service in all labors, reaches finally the highest summit of endeavor, beyond every labor, where he no longer struggles or shouts, where he ripens fully in silence, indestructibly, eternally, with the entire Universe.*

✺ 15. *There he merges with the Abyss and nestles within it like the seed of man in the womb of woman.*

✺ 16. *The Abyss is now his wife, he plows her, he opens and devours her vitals, he transmutes her blood, he laughs and weeps, he ascends and descends with her, and he never leaves her.*

✺ 17. *How can you reach the womb of the Abyss to make it fruitful? This cannot be expressed, cannot be narrowed into words, cannot be subjected to laws; every man is completely free and has his own special liberation.*

✺ 18. *No form of instruction exists, no Savior exists to open up the road. No road exists to be opened.*

❁ 19. *Every person, ascending above and beyond his own head, escapes from his small brain, so crammed with perplexities.*

❁ 20. *Within profound Silence, erect, fearless, in pain and in play, ascending ceaselessly from peak to peak, knowing that the height has no ending, sing this proud and magical incantation as you hang over the Abyss:*

I BELIEVE IN ONE GOD, DEFENDER OF THE BORDERS, OF DOUBLE DESCENT,[32] MILITANT, SUFFERING, OF MIGHTY BUT NOT OF OMNIPOTENT POWERS, A WARRIOR AT THE FARTHEST FRONTIERS, COMMANDER-IN-CHIEF OF ALL THE LUMINOUS POWERS, THE VISIBLE AND THE INVISIBLE. ❁

2 I BELIEVE IN THE INNUMERABLE, THE EPHEMERAL MASKS WHICH GOD HAS ASSUMED THROUGHOUT THE CENTURIES, AND BEHIND HIS CEASELESS FLUX I DISCERN AN INDESTRUCTIBLE UNITY. ❁

3 I BELIEVE IN HIS SLEEPLESS AND VIOLENT STRUGGLE WHICH TAMES AND FRUCTIFIES THE EARTH AS THE LIFE-GIVING FOUNTAIN OF PLANTS, ANIMALS, AND MEN. ❁

4   I BELIEVE IN MAN'S HEART, THAT EARTHEN THRESHING-FLOOR WHERE NIGHT AND DAY THE DEFENDER OF THE BORDERS FIGHTS WITH DEATH. ✿

5   O LORD, YOU SHOUT: "HELP ME! HELP ME!" YOU SHOUT, O LORD, AND I HEAR. ✿

6   WITHIN ME ALL FOREFATHERS AND ALL DESCENDANTS, ALL RACES AND ALL EARTH HEAR YOUR CRY WITH JOY AND TERROR. ✿

7   BLESSED BE ALL THOSE WHO HEAR AND RUSH TO FREE YOU, LORD, AND WHO SAY: "ONLY YOU AND I EXIST." ✿

8   BLESSED BE ALL THOSE WHO FREE YOU AND BECOME UNITED WITH YOU, LORD, AND WHO SAY: "YOU AND I ARE ONE." ✿

9   AND THRICE BLESSED BE THOSE WHO BEAR ON THEIR SHOULDERS AND DO NOT BUCKLE UNDER THIS GREAT, SUBLIME, AND TERRIFYING SECRET:

THAT EVEN THIS ONE
DOES NOT EXIST!

✿

Appendix

Acknowledgments

In September of 1954, two days after Nikos Kazantzakis and I had completed our initial study, in Greek, of *The Odyssey: A Modern Sequel*, in a skiing lodge in the French Alps above Barcelonnette, we collaborated again, on the translation of this book, *The Saviors of God*. I was fortunate to have his assistance in the explication of many difficult passages, for these *Spiritual Exercises* are a form of poetry, and consequently contain the subtleties and elusive connotations peculiar to this form. It was my great good luck to collaborate with the author, before his death, on the translations of the two books which he considered to be the heart of his life's work and on the foundations of which his subsequent fame must rest.

I am greatly indebted to Mrs. Helen Kazantzakis during this period for her hospitality, her assistance, and her constant support. I wish to thank Mr. Andonis Decavalles, the poet, and Mr. Stratis Haviaras, my assistant, for checking parts of my translation. But it is to Mr. Pandelis Prevelakis, to whom the author dedicated *The Saviors of God*, and who saw to all details pertaining to the Greek publication in its second and final form, that I am most deeply indebted. Mr. Prevelakis verified facts and dates in my introduction and, by his meticulous reading of the text, helped me to correct whatever errors remained, and to come to final decisions about several delicate shades of possible meaning. It gives me pleasure to add my dedication to that of Kazantzakis. I also wish to thank him for permission to quote from his book *Nikos Kazantzakis and His Odyssey*, published by Estia, Athens 1958, and shortly to be published by Simon and Schuster in an English translation by Philip Sherrard. I should also like to thank Mrs. Galatea Kazantzakis for permission to quote from letters addressed her by her late husband and published in *Letters to Galatea*, Diphros, Athens 1958. Most of the letters for which the source is not indicated or obvious in context were addressed to Mr. Prevelakis, and are to be found in his book.

Notes

1. In the original edition of 1927, Kazantzakis published this book with the title *Salvatores Dei* and the subtitle ΑΣΚΗΤΙΚΗ. He reversed title and subtitle in the revised edition of 1945, from which this translation was made, but I have preferred, with his permission, to keep the titular order of the first publication. The title was easy enough to translate, but the subtitle I have translated, again with his permission, as *Spiritual Exercises*, although *Ascetic* or *Asceticism* might be more literal, for the emphasis lies not so much on spiritual exercise as on spiritual *action*, though in exercise, of course, there is much of action. I have also deliberately meant to invite comparison with another great work of similar title, that by Ignatius Loyola, if only to suggest how differently two great men conceived of their spiritual and militant approach to the meaning of God.

2. *The Odyssey: A Modern Sequel* by Nikos Kazantzakis. Translation into English Verse, Introduction,

Synopsis, and Notes by Kimon Friar. Simon and Schuster, New York 1958.

3. This anecdote and the one about the Countess Enrichetta Pucci on page 28 I have taken from the journal which I kept during my stay with Kazantzakis in the summer of 1954. However, Kazantzakis had an extremely bad memory for time, place, or enumerations, and although in substance these two accounts are correct, they may have to be altered somewhat in chronology or specific detail as the facts of his life become verified.

4. *Zorba the Greek*, translated by Carl Wildman, and *The Greek Passion*, translated by Jonathan Griffin, have been reissued by Simon and Schuster in paperback, both New York 1959. The same firm has also published another novel by Kazantzakis, *Freedom or Death*, translated by Jonathan Griffin, New York 1956.

5. The quotations on pages 10–11, here slightly altered in my own translation, may be found in *The Greek Passion*, page 106, and in *Zorba the Greek*, pages 64, 113, and 134, in sequence.

6. On November 11, 1914, Kazantzakis, then thirty-one, met a young man of thirty, Anghelos Sikelianós, destined to become one of the greatest poets of modern Greece. They recognized each other immediately as kindred spirits, and three days later left for what developed into a spiritual pilgrimage of forty days throughout the monasteries on the "Holy Mountain" of Athos. On November 29, in the monastery of Karakálou, Kazantzakis wrote in his journal: "In our beds [Sikelianós and I] talked about the essence of our highest desires: to create religion. Everything made mature! Ah! how to manifest whatever we possess within us which is most profound and most holy!" On December 8, in the monastery of St. Paul, he wrote: "Today I was deeply moved by Tolstoy. His tragic flight—a confession of defeat. He wanted to create religion, but could only create novels and literature. His deepest essence—he knew this well—never found expression." Later, in

October of 1915, he noted: "I am reading a biography of Tolstoy. I am always moved by his spiritual elevation; literature was never enough for him. He had need for religion. I should start from where Tolstoy left off." On July 1915 he left alone for the island of Siphnos and lived in a cell in the monastery of The Madonna of the Mountains. Between the twelfth and the eighteenth of that month, he was writing in furious haste: "I write and write, the floodgates have burst, the knot has loosened, the gasping has stopped! I feel disburdened, happy, as though I'd never known the world. Locked in my cell, alone with the alone, face to face with myself." . . . "At noon on the eighteenth I finished my book. It's only the skeleton, but I feel lightened, because I wrote it with absolute sincerity. Immediately after, I fell sick, with fever and vomiting."

I have taken these notations from a detailed chronology of Kazantzakis' life made by Mr. Pandelis Prevelakis and presented by him in the Memorial Volume for Kazantzakis published by Nea Estia, Athens, as a special Christmas issue in 1959. Mr. Prevelakis conjectures that the work which Kazantzakis wrote with such feverish haste was *The Holy Mountain*, which, in October 1915, he listed as among his works, and which was probably the original very rough outline of *The Saviors of God*. In his Mt. Athos journal, dated November–December 1914, Kazantzakis had noted that he planned to write a book about his "spiritual pilgrimage" with Sikelianós, of "how we lived our race, the faith of our fathers, how everywhere we elevated the spirit, how we hailed that life which soars toward heaven like an arrow of divine grace [See *The Odyssey: A Modern Sequel*, Book XV, 1173–1176] . . . How I read Dante, Buddha, the Gospels."

7. See *The Odyssey*, Book X, 699–701.

8. Book XVI, 959.

9. For the latter part of the letter of March 1923, see section "The Relationship Between God and Man"

of this book. See also *The Odyssey*, Book XV, 864–964.

10. In the edition of 1945, the section "Ancestor." was retitled "The Race."

11. Verse 38.

12. See *The Odyssey*, Book XV, 801–863.

13. See *The Odyssey*, "Prologue," 23–30; also "The Relationship Between God and Man," Verse 47 of this book.

14. The reader will find the material of this letter scattered throughout many sections of *The Saviors of God*. Although this book is the key to all of Kazantzakis' work, the ideas are most fully embodied in *The Odyssey*, particularly in Books XIV–XVI, XVIII, XXIII. Much of *The Saviors of God* was also embodied in a novel. *Le Jardin des Rochers*, which Kazantzakis wrote in French; this was published by Werelbibliotheek, Amsterdam 1939, and in Spanish translation by Ercilla, Santiago, Chile, 1941. This novel was recently translated into Greek by Mr. Pandelis Prevelakis.

15. For a fuller analysis of the relationship between writers of epic and the problem of myth, see my essay "Myth and Metaphysics: An Introduction to Modern Poetry," in *Modern Poetry: American and British*, edited by Kimon Friar and John Malcolm Brinnin, Appleton-Century-Crofts, New York 1951.

16. In 1939 in Athens, a few years after the publication of *The Saviors of God*, Kazantzakis was accused of atheism, and his trial set for June 10; but he was never summoned. Fourteen years later, in 1953, when he was writing his novelized life of St. Francis, the Greek Orthodox Church sought to persecute him for several pages of *Freedom or Death*, and for his entire conception of *The Last Temptation of Christ*, even though the latter work had as yet appeared in German only, and not in Greek. This agitation continued throughout the following year. In April 1954, when the Pope placed *The Last Temptation of Christ* on the Index, Kazantza-

kis telegraphed the Committee of the Index a sentence from Tertullian: "*Ad tuum, Domine, tribunal, appello.*" He added the following note: "I address the same sentence also to the Greek Orthodox Church, 'At your tribunal, Lord, I make my appeal.' For our own Metropolitans and Bishops I add the following: 'Holy Fathers, you gave me a curse, but I give you a blessing. May your conscience be as pure as mine, and may you be as moral and as religious as I.'"

17. *Zorba*, page 185.

18. To be published by Simon and Schuster in the fall of 1960.

19. *The Odyssey*, Book XXI, 1277.

20. For the conversation between Odysseus, Margaro and Prince Motherth, see *The Odyssey*, Book XVIII, 1097–1219.

21. The story about the well is told in *Zorba the Greek*, pages 174–175.

22. See *The Odyssey*, Book XVIII, 1222–34.

23. See *The Odyssey*, Book XVIII, 899–904.

24. See also Verse 37 of "The Preparation, Third Duty." For an equally appropriate epitaph, written by Kazantzakis for his autobiographical hero Odysseus, which I should like to see one day engraved for himself, in marble above his grave, see *The Odyssey*, Book XXII, 27–37:

> Let Death come down to slavish souls and
>   craven heads
> with his sharp scythe and barren bones, but let
>   him come
> to this lone man like a great lord to knock with
>   shame
> on his five famous castle doors, and with great
>   awe
> plunder whatever dregs in his life's dreadful
>   strife
> have not found time to turn in his strong body
>   from flesh

and bone into pure spirit, lightning, joy and
 deeds.
The Archer has fooled you, Death, he's squan-
 dered all your goods,
melted down all the rusts and rots of his foul
 flesh
till they escaped you in pure spirit, for when
 you come,
you'll find but trampled fires, embers, ash, and
 fleshly dross.

25. See *The Odyssey*, Book XXVI, 1180.

26. See *The Odyssey*, Book XIX, 257–258.

27. The reader is referred to my Introduction in *The Odyssey* for a short synopsis of *The Saviors of God* and for a fuller account of the influence of Nietzsche and Bergson on Kazantzakis' thought and style.

28. See *The Odyssey*, page xxvi.

29. See *The Odyssey*, Book XIII, 1237–46.

30. Spirit: The Greek word is πνοή, meaning "breath," but it is also the root word of πνεῦμα, meaning "spirit," somewhat similar to the relationship in English between "inspire" (to breathe) and "inspiration." I thought it best here and in more central passages of the text, where the word is capitalized by Kazantzakis, to translate "spirit," which, of course, derives from the Latin *spiritus* meaning "breath." I wish to stress, however, that the word "spirit" is not to be equated with "soul," but rather with Bergson's *élan vital*, with the life principle which animates all of nature. See especially Verses 38–40 of "The Vision," Verses 9–12 of "The Relationship Between God and Man," and also Verse 16 of "The Relationship Between Man and Man" where I have translated "It is the spirit, the breathing of God on earth," whereas the literal translation would be "It is the breath, the respiration of God on earth."

31. *Rose of the Winds*: The card of the mariner's compass, so called because of its roseate design.

32. *Defender of the Borders, of Double Descent*:
This refers in particular to Vasílius Diyenís Akrítas, a
tenth-century Byzantine hero. *Diyenís* means "of double birth," for Akrítas' father was a Moslem and his
mother a Christian Greek. *Akrítas* means "border
guard" of the Empire.

About the Author

The late NIKOS KAZANTZAKIS, acclaimed as one of the great writers of modern Europe, was born in Crete in 1883 and studied at the University of Athens as well as under the philosopher Henri Bergson in Paris. After extensive travel, he settled on the island of Aegina during World War II, where he devoted himself to literary and philosophical work. His writings include some ten novels, ten dramas, five books of travel, five of *belles lettres* and one of poetry. In addition, he has translated into modern Greek verse Homer's *Iliad* and *Odyssey*, Dante's *Divine Comedy* and Goethe's *Faust*. In the United States, he is best known as the author of the widely acclaimed novels *Zorba the Greek* and *The Greek Passion* (made into a distinguished film under .the title of "He Who Must Die"), and for his monumental epic, *The Odyssey: A Modern Sequel*, which was published in this country in 1958 and won immediate acclaim as a masterpiece of world literature.

About the Translator

KIMON FRIAR, poet and scholar, was born on an island in the Sea of Marmara that was settled by Jason's Argonauts, and came to the United States at an early age. He began his career as a translator at the University of Michigan, and later taught at several universities. In 1954 he became the Fulbright Research Scholar in Modern Greek Literature at the University of Athens. For four years he directed the famous Poetry Center in New York City, and has been a steady contributor to many periodicals and anthologies. His most impressive work to date has been his translation of *The Odyssey: A Modern Sequel*, which was hailed as a creative achievement in its own right. His future plans include an anthology of his translations, *Contemporary Greek Poets*, and a long poem of his own.

14 DAY BOOK

Wilmington Public Library
Wilmington, N. C.

RULES

1. Books marked 7 days may be kept one week. Books marked 14 days, two weeks. The latter may be renewed, if more than 6 months old.

2. A fine of two cents a day will be charged on each book which is not returned according to the above rule. No book will be issued to any person having a fine of 25 cents or over.

3. A charge of ten cents will be made for mutilated plastic jackets. All injuries to books beyond reasonable wear and all losses shall be made good to the satisfaction of the Librarian.

4. Each borrower is held responsible for all books drawn on his card and for all fines accruing on the same.